The Passion for Success

The Mindset of Champions

David Roy Eaton

THE
PASSION
FUND

www.thepassionfund.com

Published in Boca Raton, Florida by The Passion Fund
www.thepassionfund.com

All Scripture quotations, unless otherwise indicated, are taken from the Holy Bible, New International Version (NIV). Copyright ©1973, 1978, 1984, International Bible Society. Used by permission of Zondervan Bible Publishers.

THE PASSION FOR SUCCESS

Printed in the United States of America

1 2 3 4 5 6 — 10 09 08 07 06

Contents

About the Author

David Roy Eaton, a graduate of Princeton University, was headed for a career in medicine until a friend introduced him to the financial industry. He now serves as Chairman and CEO of The Eaton Group, a wealth accumulation and distribution strategy firm with offices in New York City and Boca Raton, Florida. As a personal finance expert, he has been an advisor to high net-worth individuals and family-owned businesses for more than twenty years. David has appeared on CNN, CNN-FN, NY-1, CNBC, and Fox News. His articles have been published in *The New York Times, Crain's New York Business,* and *Black Enterprise.*

David is also the founder of Life's Passions Events Planning, LLC, a consulting firm dedicated to creating transformational experiences for high achievers and unique events for the philanthropic community. His charitable pursuits include serving as development consultant for The American Cancer Society, board member for Friends of Island Academy, former board member of the Associated Black Charities, Benefit Committee member for The Fresh Air Fund, development consultant to The Arthur Ashe Institute for Urban Health, Tennis Pro for the New York Junior Tennis League, and member of the Planned Giving and Endowments for the UJA-Federation.

A master of the art of networking and a dynamic public speaker, David has facilitated seminar workshops for several organizations, including The Practicing Law Institute, Thelen Reid and Priest LLP, IBM, The Guardian Life Insurance Elite Conference, Cushman and Wakefield, Credit Suisse, and CB Richard Ellis.

An avid tennis player and instructor, David enjoys serving as a personal coach on and off the court.

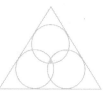

Foreword

I have been a financial advisor for more than twenty-two years. When I entered the life insurance business, I thought meeting the rich and famous and being their financial guru would be fun. My assumption was that people with megawealth were happy, excited about life, and very generous with both their time and money.

I was greatly mistaken.

As I became increasingly frustrated with the selfish, greedy, and egotistical people who had a lot of money, I decided to search for the true source of happiness. I interviewed 513 individuals with a liquid net worth of at least $10 million to determine whether money has any relationship to happiness in life. I spent five years doing research and meeting with some of the most powerful people in America.

The subjects ranged in age from late twenties to early seventies. Thirty percent had inherited their wealth, and seventy percent were self-made deca-millionaires. Several of the younger subjects had made their money in the dot-com boom of the 1990s. One subject retired at age fifty to pursue a life of philanthropy.

The advice in this book is based on the best practices of the five percent of the ultra-affluent people I interviewed who led balanced lives. Profile descriptions of eleven of these individuals are presented throughout the book. The following diagram illustrates how I define living a balanced life, which I call, "living in the delta."

The American paradigm is that when you become rich, happiness follows. We see successful business people such as Donald Trump and Martha Stewart achieving fame and wealth and

The Passion Triangle

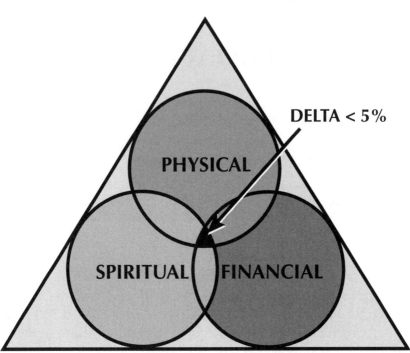

DELTA < 5%

PHYSICAL

SPIRITUAL   FINANCIAL

assume they're happy. But how much is enough? What are the lives of the rich really like behind all of the fame and money?

I asked all of the subjects of my sociological experiment ten questions:

1. Are you happy?
2. How do you define happiness?
3. Are you successful?
4. How do you define success?
5. What is your greatest accomplishment in life?
6. What are your strengths?
7. What are your weaknesses?
8. If you were to live your life over again, what would you do differently?
9. What is your purpose in life?
10. How do you want to be remembered when you are no longer alive?

I then compiled the data and looked for trends. Ninety-five percent of the subjects described their success in life in terms of money and material possessions. I define these individuals as the *rich*. There were distinctly different answers from those I define as *wealthy*. To be a member of the Five-Percent Club is an extraordinary accomplishment. It requires constantly reinforcing your character and your inner strength through spiritual practices. To transform from being rich to being wealthy requires a sincere desire to help others and often follows a catastrophic or life-altering event, such as the death of a child, close friend, or spouse; an emotionally or physically abusive relationship; or a near-death experience.

For me, the rock-bottom moment was losing more than $500,000 in a nine-month period playing craps in casinos in Atlantic City, Las Vegas, and New Orleans. The essence of life became very clear to me in my time of despair. I was put on earth to make the lives of all those I touch as wonderful as possible by being the kind of person I would like to see in the world. Mahatma Gandhi said, "Be the change you want to see in the world." I live my life by those words every day and attract some extraordinary people as a result.

The Passion for Success: The Mindset of Champions is designed to be a wake up call to those who fit (or aspire to) the deca-millionaire profile. I want you to question the American paradigm that money will take care of all other deficiencies (i.e., you will be generous, spend time with family, and explore your passions in life once you are rich). We spend far too much attention and time focusing on the lifestyles of the rich and famous and not enough time becoming well-rounded human beings. None of the people I interviewed said that they wish they had worked harder in their lives.

I have failed in business and sales several times, and I would like to thank God for giving me the challenges that allowed me to test my character and resourcefulness. The adversity has made me a stronger person because I knew that if I could make it through "X," my ordinary challenges are relatively minor. I played it safe for the first thirty-six years in life, and then I decided to take a chance and live life "full-throttle."

I am making my HYPHEN *ROCK* (see page 32), and I invite you to join me on this journey toward nirvana. I suggest various exercises and practices through the book. They are not meant to be truth or an absolute answer. They are experiences that have helped me and the five percent of survey respondents to lead balanced lives. Please read the acknowledgments at the end of every chapter to see the inspiration for the subject matter. I've listed five people whose contributions to my life are related to the title for each chapter.

I welcome your feedback as you apply the principles of *The Passion for Success: The Mindset of Champions* in your everyday life. Knowledge without execution is incomplete.

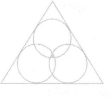

Introduction

We have all been given an incredible gift—the gift of life. For me, the million-dollar question is: "What am I doing with this gift?"

As you read *The Passion for Success*, you will learn how I am answering this question for myself. My ultimate objective in writing this book, however, is to inspire you to provide your own answer to this question.

I suggest that how we choose to live our lives is what really separates the "haves" from the "have nots." Which are you? Before you answer that question, let's define *have*. Does it mean you:

- have money?
- are rich?
- are wealthy?

For my definitions of *have*, *have not*, *rich*, and *wealthy*, keep reading! I will share with you what I believe it means to "have it all," to be *wealthy* instead of *rich* and to pursue your passions in order to lead a more successful, fulfilling life.

First, let me share my background so you will understand my perspective on these subjects. I have counseled clients, lawyers, CPAs, and numerous other financial and investment professionals about insurance for over twenty years. Throughout my career, I have been introduced to literally thousands of individuals who, by most of our definitions, have *a lot* of money (several million dollars). But, while we may classify these individuals as *rich,* I consider only a select few to be *wealthy*, as I define this word for myself.

In the course of my work, charity, and daily life, discussions about money, wealth, family, happiness, the meaning of life, and success inevitably occur quite frequently. Many of the people I meet tell me they will be happy when they have more money. Yet, ironically, most of the "rich" people I meet (those high net worth individuals with several million dollars) are no happier in their lives than their lower net worth counterparts.

Over the years I began to ask myself:

- If money can't buy happiness, how do we achieve happiness?
- If having money isn't an accurate measure of success in life, what is?
- What is a wealthy life?

By sharing my answers to these questions with you, I intend to prompt you to take stock of how you have been spending life's most valuable currency, your time. After gaining a fresh perspective and perhaps a few new insights, you may choose to rebalance the amount of time you invest in each area of your Life Plan Portfolio (just as you should evaluate and redistribute the investments in your financial portfolio each year).

When was the last time you took a look at what's in your Life Plan Portfolio? Are you where you intended to be at this point in your life with regard to your:

- Health?
- Marriage or a significant relationship?
- Relationships with your children, grandchildren, parents, siblings, and friends?
- Career or business?
- Investments/financial net worth?
- Toys (cars, boats, planes, vacation homes)?
- Charitable activities and level of giving?
- Life's passions?
- Personal and spiritual growth?
- Overall level of contentment?

I want to make you think BIG . . .

If you are a student or just starting out, I hope you will use *The Passion for Success* as a reference book to build the life you want for yourself. Although achieving success in life requires hard work, focus, and dedication, it should also be fun all along the way.

If you are nearing retirement or are already retired, I want you to think about the most gratifying times in your life. How would you compare how you felt during those times to how you feel right now? If this is the best time of your life, good for you! If it's not, I hope reading *The Passion for Success* will reawaken something within you and stir you to pursue the people and passions you value most. With maturity, experience, and resources, you will have all that you need to live life on your own terms.

For everyone in the middle stages of life, *The Passion for Success* offers tools to help you evaluate, reevaluate, reinvent, redefine, discover, and rediscover what it means to really live your life. Do you want to merely struggle and survive? Or do you want to know what it will take to finally arrive and thrive?

Whether you read one chapter a day or each week, you'll need to allow time for each idea to sprout from its seed, take root in your mind, and grow as you put the concepts to use in your daily life.

So, how do I know these ideas work? Because I am sharing the success practices that helped me graduate from an Ivy League college, earn a seven-figure income as a top producer for a major life insurance firm, and allow me to pursue my life passions, including playing tennis at a competitive level nearly every day.

The sources of many of the life knowledge nuggets examined in *The Passion for Success* are the wise people whom I have been most fortunate to call my family and friends. My Circle of Success includes my parents, my paternal grandmother, a former business partner, several of my successful "wealthy" clients and associates, as well as some very special people who have crossed my path as life teachers and friends.

While each chapter stands on its own, I wrote each one with a certain progression of thought in mind. So, when you read this book for the first time, I suggest following the chapters in sequence. Completing the exercises (questions) at the end of each chapter will personalize the material for you. And I encourage you to refer back to each chapter as you would a reference book, until the new ideas on these pages really begin to take shape for you as you apply them in your own life.

I can't wait to serve up the first course!

So, to whet your appetite, here is a brief description of what you will learn in each upcoming chapter of *The Passion for Success:*

"10 Keys to Independence" offers a concise, how-to guide to attaining personal, professional, and financial freedom via the ten specific steps I teach my clients to practice in their daily lives.

"What is Passion?" explores one of my favorite subjects and the inspiration for the title of this book, the power of passion. In my opinion, the word *passion* is one of the most misunderstood and underappreciated words in the English language. It is too often narrowly defined as sexual desire, yet it has a spiritual context and a much broader definition of "boundless enthusiasm." Examine what gets you excited. What could you spend your time doing 365 days a year, twenty-four hours a day, seven days a week and still want "just five more minutes?" What really stirs you up and gives you that feeling you get when you are in the moment, in the zone, have no worries, and can't get enough? For me, it's tennis and dancing!

"What is Success?" delves into the topic of what it means to be successful. I work with many young people who often tell me they "wanna be successful." So what is success? Is it having lots of money? Is it being an important person? Is it having your own business? Is it being really smart? Is it having a good family? We will measure success in three levels: spiritual, physical, and financial.

"Power of Team" presents a paradigm shift for many Americans because the emphasis is on achieving success through team—rather than individual—effort. Whether you have aspirations to climb the corporate ladder or are striving to preserve/improve your family relationships (your home team), this is a must-read.

"Finding Your Purpose in Life" challenges you to stop and

think about why you are on this earth. Too many people spend all their time working or earning a living without thought to *why they're here* or *what they want* to do with their lives. It's never too late to stop and answer these all-important questions.

"Happiness vs. Contentment" looks at the differences between these familiar terms. Since everyone wants to be happy in life, I'll ask you to define these words. Are you really seeking happiness, or is contentment what you desire? How can you achieve these seemingly elusive states of being?

"Focus" examines the ability to focus, one of the most powerful skills successful people possess. Individuals who have mastered this discipline are able to tune out distractions encountered in daily life. They pursue their goals with sheer determination and single-minded purpose. Their starting points are clearly defined intentions with predetermined pathways to the finish line, which is the accomplishment of each stated objective.

"Dancing with Life" teaches you how to develop a deeper awareness of the more subtle rhythms of life. It's about observation, listening, and communication. We all have our own style, our unique "dance." When we want to connect with friends, coworkers, or spouses, we need to establish a rapport so we can dance together—without stepping on each other's toes! The key is figuring out how to dance in sync with your partner.

"Philanthropy as a Passion" considers the human desire to make a difference in the world, what it feels like when we do good things, and why this is so important. What motivates you to take action? Feelings about an injustice, the loss of a loved one, a health crisis, a global catastrophe? Would you give your time or money because you believe in a cause such as furthering education, feeding the poor, protecting the environment, or preserving the arts?

"Overcoming Fear" deals with conquering the negative forces of fear in our lives. Once we learn to recognize how fear insidiously manifests itself in numerous aspects of our day-to-day lives, we can work on learning how to conquer this self-limiting and destructive state of mind.

"Exercises to Build the Self-Confidence Muscle" reflects on

the value of possessing a healthy self-confidence (not to be con-fused with a false sense of self, arrogance, or boastfulness). How you see yourself is so important to your success, yet, ironically, most people do not possess true self-confidence until after they have attained some measure of achievement. This chapter intro-duces what I call the "Fonzie exercise." You'll need a mirror and a calendar for this one!

"Taking risk" ventures into the big leagues, where the sport of risk-taking separates life's winners from the also-rans. For many, taking a risk is heart stopping, but for entrepreneurs and leaders alike, it gets the heart pumping and the blood flowing. One of the keys to developing a tolerance for risk is learning how to assess and manage risk so you remain in control no mat-ter the outcome.

"Faith" addresses one of the most empowering and contro-versial personal and cultural forces shaping us as individuals and as a society: our faith. Rather than discuss faith in the con-text of any religion, we will concentrate on the aspects of faith that call upon our inner resources, strength and beliefs, all of which are needed to grow and achieve our own greatness.

"Empowerment" scrutinizes our collective sense of entitle-ment and takes a critical look at the dysfunction present throughout our well-intentioned social welfare system. This chapter is meant to stimulate reevaluation of what actually pro-motes independence and self-reliance, and how we need to fos-ter a guided process of letting go—of our children, families, friends, and everyone else who looks to us for a helping hand.

"Circle of Success" helps you take a 360-degree look at the people around you. Your family, friends, and associates are your circle of influence; their values, attitudes, and worldviews have a profound impact on your life. You need to take great care to cultivate a Circle of Success—people who will elevate you, rather than bring you down to their level.

"Acknowledgment" is about acknowledging the people in your life—often. You will notice that I end each chapter of this book by thanking the individuals who served as inspiration for the content. Expressing your gratitude doesn't need to be for-mal; a simple "thank you" or compliment is usually enough to make someone feel appreciated. Acknowledging all the people who help you is critical to your success.

"Health, Vitality, and Fitness" goes beyond an obligatory mention of the necessary roles health, vitality, and fitness play in each of our lives. In this chapter, I demand that you focus as much attention on this area of your life as you do on your work life.

"Children as Masters of Life and Teachers of Truth" celebrates the greatest life forces (and most valuable resource) on our planet: children. To know what I'm talking about, watch your children at play; listen to what they say. Consider what it would be like if you could live your adult life as you did when you were a child. I bet you would feel less self-conscious and constrained. You'd probably feel free of worry and doubt—and your life would be a lot more fun.

"Creating an Extraordinary Future" encourages you to expend the extra effort necessary to create an extraordinary life and not settle for an ordinary life.

The message I want you to receive as you read every page of this book is that it's not too late to wake up and discover what it means to really live life on your own terms. What are your life passions? What stands in your way of going for your dreams?

I hope *The Passion for Success* leads you to find personal success, peace of mind, and your own path toward a wealthy life.

Exercises

1. What are the top three areas in life you want to master?
2. Ask three friends for their definitions of financial success.
3. Write down the top three results you want to achieve in your life upon completion of this book.

For their inspiration and guidance with the material in this chapter, many thanks go to:

Bernice Eaton (Grandma). For teaching me to believe that anything is possible.

Roy Eaton (Dad). For being my spiritual mentor.

Minnette Eaton (Mom). For showing me unconditional love.

Scott Silbert (Former Business Partner). For teaching me responsibility and partnership.

Walter Delph, M.D. (Uncle). For exposing me to the finer things in life.

CHAPTER 1

10 Keys
to Independence

Wouldn't it be great to have the freedom to spend money on anything you want, go anywhere you want to go, and do whatever you want to do? You can, anytime you are ready—because you have the keys to your own independence. You just have to remember where you put them!

If you are like every other human on the planet, your set of keys is locked up inside you. Personal, professional, and financial independence starts in your mind. It is really about the internal relationship you have with yourself. If you're weighed down worrying about the past, your job, your kids, or other issues, there is no way you can dedicate the energy and effort needed to move toward the life you really want.

Remember, a basic tenet of every faith is trusting your higher power to show you how to achieve what you want. You may not always receive what you ask for in the exact way you envisioned, but life will work out as long as you strive to do right by others and yourself.

That being said, let's find your 10 Keys to Independence:

1. Live in the moment.

One of the best ways to create the level of focus necessary to live in the moment is to meditate. Meditation is about clearing your mind and getting centered. It's quite simple, but it demands discipline.

There are many different forms of meditation and "getting

centered." For some people (like me) the practice and discipline of yoga is the best route to learning how to live in the moment.

My father has always been a big a proponent of Transcendental Meditation (TM). You can sign up for a course, where they will teach you a mantra, breathing techniques, and sitting position, and they make sure you're practicing it correctly.

2. Create an exciting vision of the future.

This is a four-question process that I recommend for every person reading this book:

Question #1: *How do you envision your life three years from now?*

Close your eyes and envision your life three years from now (in as detailed a manner as possible).

For example, if you want to be living in a new house, how many rooms does it have? What are the colors you've chosen for each room? Does it have a pool? What does the neighborhood look like?

If you are seeking a relationship, what will this person look like (what color hair, eyes, skin)? How tall? How old? What are his or her interests?

Think about your career or your plans for traveling around the world, and fill in all the details. You must complete this visualization process for all areas of the life you want for yourself.

It is essential to be as specific as possible. You can't say, "I want to have a lot of money." You need to specify exactly how much money you will have in three years: "I will have $5 million by June 1, 2009." Then you need to indicate how much money will be in CDs, stocks, bonds, real estate, your checking account, and so on.

I did this exercise three years before I made a million dollars. I said, "I want a million dollars." I put it out there, and I created it.

As you complete this exercise, you are creating your plan (starting with the specific actions you must begin taking today) to achieve the life you envision having three years from now.

Question #2: *What are the top three obstacles to attaining your goals?*

For me, I struggled with procrastination, lack of financial discipline, and putting too much of my energy into unhealthy relationships.

Question #3: *What assets already exist that could help you realize the life you want for yourself in three years?*

Some of my assets include being an alumnus of Princeton University, a tennis professional, and a successful entrepreneur.

Question #4: *What top three personal strengths could you focus on to guarantee the realization of your dreams?*

We spend far too much time and energy trying to make up for our weaknesses. Identify what it is that you're great at and work to become even better at it. Michael Jordan was great at his jump shots and dunking, so he spent most of his time perfecting jump shots and dunking. The great athletes all follow this principle.

3. Surround yourself with people who have what you want.

Five years from now you will have become like the people with whom you associate today. Once you get clear on what it is you want to attain, search for the people who already have it and surround yourself with those types of people. Model yourself after them: dine at the restaurants, join the gyms, and attend the events where you will find the type of person you aspire to become. Read the same books and newspapers they read, watch the same television programs, and attend the same plays.

As you become a familiar face to the people with whom you would like to associate, you will eventually create the opportunity to play a game of tennis, have a drink, or do business together.

Take on business partners (or team members at work) who have qualities you want to develop in yourself. In fact, seek individuals who are two to three levels ahead of you. Over time you will become like the people you associate with because you'll take on their habits. (This is why parents are concerned about the schools their children attend and the friends they bring home.)

4. Keep your word.

There is an oft-quoted passage from the Bible that says, "In the beginning was the Word" (John 1:1). All we really have is what we say. So, if you promise X, deliver X. I guarantee that if you follow this simple advice you will have more business than you can imagine. You will also have relationships that work because people will regard you as someone they can trust.

Back when I was taking my first steps toward becoming successful, I kept track of all the things I didn't do right by writing them down so I could correct myself. When I caught myself saying something I knew wasn't going to happen, I would apologize and correct myself.

For example, instead of telling someone I would meet them at 11:00 a.m. because I knew that was what they wanted to hear (but at the same time I knew I couldn't get there until 11:30 a.m.), I would say, "You know what? I am sorry, and I know this won't make you happy, but I really can't be there until 11:30 a.m." I learned that most people respect honesty.

Don't make promises you can't keep, and don't give yourself wiggle room. This customer service policy helped to build Mitchell's, a prominent men's clothing store in Westport, Connecticut, with a clientele that includes a "Who's Who" of CEOs and top executives from Fortune 500 companies including Chase, GE, IBM, Merrill Lynch, and Pepsi. Jack Mitchell, son of the founder, wrote a terrific book about customer service, *Hug Your Customers*. He credits the store's success to building a reputation for always delivering what was promised.

5. Make unreasonable requests.

There's a story about a pastor who wanted to build a spectacular church and needed to raise the money to build it. So he created a plan of action and made requests—even unreasonable requests—for donations. He succeeded in raising the money and building the cathedral. You may have heard of this pastor—his name is Dr. Robert Schuller.

Too many people are afraid to ask for what they want or need. This is especially common among average salespeople who make presentations but never ask for the sale. They make the mistake of anticipating the "no" before they even ask the question. What do you think their outcomes will be? If they don't ask the question, the answer is "no" by default.

As a top-producing sales agent and fundraiser, I know you need to be willing to be rejected and called crazy or even more colorful adjectives. You need to remember when someone says "no," they aren't rejecting you; they just don't want to give to your project or buy your product.

We are our own worst enemies because we allow ourselves to be fearful. As President Franklin Roosevelt said, "The only thing we have to fear is fear itself."

If you want to accomplish great things and have an extraordinary life, you need to take risks. You will inevitably (and often) fail, but what counts is the eventual achievement of your desired result. You will meet with success—but only if you put yourself out there.

6. Give with no expectation of getting.

There are so many people who give to get. "If I give $1 million to the museum, they'll name a building after me . . . "

The act of giving is, ultimately, the act of getting: "A merciful man doeth good to his own soul" (Proverbs 11:17).

I'm suggesting that giving to get something in return is not true philanthropy. In my mind, the purest form of philanthropy is giving as an anonymous donor.

7. Take action consistent with your vision.

I was always very good at planning and goal setting. But I needed to work on my ability to take action, so I enlisted help to strengthen myself in this area. I have surrounded myself with some tough people who are willing to call me on the carpet when I don't do what I say I'm going to do.

My right-hand man, Gregg Epstein, will ask me questions like: "Did you call this person?" and "You said you were going to send in that application, when are you going to do it?"

Even though I complain at times that he is a real pain in the neck, I am thankful he is in my life.

One of my friends knew a writer who was suffering from writer's block. The writer made a commitment to write one thousand words first thing, every single day, because once you get in the practice of writing (or performing any task), you form the habit. When you have established a new habit, it becomes easier to get the job done because everything will flow automatically—especially when your mind (your biggest obstacle) gets out of your way.

8. Trust in a Higher Power.

If you believe in God (or a Higher Power), then you will understand that God places messages somewhere inside of you. If you believe God gave you the idea you could do or be something, then you need to ask:

- How do I get from here to there?
- What kind of actions do I need to take?
- What kind of person do I need to be?
- What kind of people do I need to surround myself with?
- What should my focus be?

Then you have to listen and watch for the answers. You will receive the lessons life presents through nature and your environment—which include the people you meet, books you read, and daily meditation. If you have your eyes and consciousness open (which is what meditation enables you to do), you will see that all of the answers you need are present.

The only other question I have for you is this: Do you have your hearing aid turned on? I use the metaphor of the hearing aid all the time, but I really should be asking if you have your "listening" aid on. Although most of us are fortunate enough to have our hearing, we often fail to listen because listening requires our active participation.

Successful people have developed the skill of listening.

9. Be enthusiastic.

There is nothing more powerful than being enthusiastic. Enthusiasm is contagious. If you are passionate about something you are doing in life, you will attract people who will just want to be around you. Enthusiasm (like passion) can be spiritually based.

Remember Tiger Woods when he first came onto the professional golf scene? Fans loved to watch him get pumped up as he was winning; they loved his drive and intensity.

Think of all the great basketball coaches who stand on the sidelines of the court, gesturing, cheering, and pulling for their teams to win. They have tremendous enthusiasm and passion for the game and their players' success.

I can't tell you exactly what it is that gets me so excited about playing tennis. But I'm learning that I can choose to become enthusiastic about things that I am not as naturally excited about doing, too.

There are circumstances where you need to be more creative or effective, perhaps more focused than you feel. In these situations you can close your eyes and create an environment in which you can summon that enthusiasm or passion or power of concentration.

Several years ago I participated in a personal development seminar that focused on some very intense self-work. Afterward, the facilitator prompted us to "close our eyes and go to the beach and play like a kid."

Can you close your eyes and go to the beach to play? Try to visualize an infinite space filled with nothing but white sand and the sounds and smells of the blue ocean with its waves lapping upon the shore. Now, imagine yourself relaxing on a comfortable lounge chair soaking up the warmth and light of the sun as the cool breeze blows in from offshore.

When you visualize the beach or any scenario that gives you

pleasure, you can create a powerful intention which is far more effective than reacting out of stress, fear, worry, or doubt—not the optimum place from which to generate a vision!

Therefore, there is a whole mental game to generating enthusiasm and passion.

10. Be persistent.

Calvin Coolidge once said, "Nothing in the world can take the place of persistence. Talent will not; nothing is more common than unsuccessful men with talent. Genius will not; unrewarded genius is almost a proverb. Education will not; the world is full of educated derelicts. Persistence and determination are omnipotent. The slogan 'press on' has solved and always will solve the problems of the human race."

Think about it. There are many talented people who are derelicts! There are geniuses driving taxicabs and very well educated people who can't get jobs. So achieving success and independence requires more than brainpower alone. Rather, it takes a single-mindedness of purpose.

Thomas Edison is a perfect example of the power of persistence—he failed over a thousand times before he succeeded with his invention of the electric light bulb. We might all still be sitting in the dark if Edison had given up after the five hundredth failure!

Be sure to include Lance Armstrong as a model for persistence—physically and mentally. This man fought his way back from cancer and won the Tour de France bicycle race on more than one occasion. Cancer would have meant retirement for just about anyone else.

Once you have established your goals and objectives, you need to put your plan in place. Your plan is your foundation; it is the structure you need to support your efforts as you pursue your objectives.

Let me share one more personal example about persistence with you:

One of my biggest life insurance clients is someone whom I first did business with back in 1990. That initial sale was a pretty big deal for me at the time. And, since it was my job to maintain ongoing relationships with my clients, I would call upon this client in order to do an annual review (to stay informed of changes that go on in the client's life and adjust the insurance strategies). I called him once a week for two and a half years before he actually returned my phone calls.

When he finally spoke with me, we did a deal four times the size of our original deal.

I then called to check in with him after another six months passed, just to keep in touch. I called him every week, and he didn't return my phone calls. Another two years passed. Then he called me back, and we did an even larger deal!

Now would you agree that the average person would have stopped calling the client after the first call, second call, fifth call, or hundredth call?

Persistence is the key that will ultimately unlock the door and set you free. If you know what you want and you are persistent, you will eventually get the deals. But sometimes you need to stay on 'em like a pit bull!

I hope this chapter helped you understand that independence is a state of mind that starts from within. Once you are free within, you will be able to live in the moment. When you are a truly independent and complete person, you will be able to attract others who are also complete.

Envision your life as you want it, and write down the actions you need to take to make it all happen. Be sure to enlist the help of those who will support you as you strive to accomplish your life goals (and don't be afraid to make unreasonable requests).

In closing, I suggest that you review your goals and life plan every three months. It is human nature to put off taking the actions needed to achieve your goals until the last minute. If you wait, it will be too late.

David's 10 Keys to Independence:

1. Live in the moment.
2. Create an exciting vision of the future.

3. Surround yourself with people who have what you want.
4. Keep your word.
5. Make unreasonable requests.
6. Give with no expectation of getting.
7. Take action every day consistent with your vision.
8. Trust in a Higher Power.
9. Be enthusiastic.
10. Be persistent.

Exercises

1. Answer the questions on pages 20–21 in detail.
2. Each day for fourteen days, close your eyes and focus on your breathing; inhale for a count of two, hold for a count of ten and exhale for a count of four. Repeat the exercise for ten minutes.
3. Make two unreasonable requests for fourteen consecutive days and record your experiences and emotions.

For their inspiration and guidance with the material in this chapter, many thanks go to:

Werner Erhard. For creating the *est* training and beginning my self-development journey.

Sid Dinerstein. For unwavering commitment to your passions and political guidance.

Boca Raton Resort & Club. For creating paradise on earth and allowing me to experience inner peace.

Dan Kern. For providing a NYC office out of generosity.

Stephen Covey. For writing *The Seven Habits of Highly Effective People* and creating powerful distinctions.

Wealthy Profile #1

Restaurateur, 46, married, living in New York City with a fifteen-year-old daughter and a thirteen-year-old son. He followed his passion for wine and fine dining and created several of the most popular restaurants in New York City's history. His attention to detail and customer service are unparalleled. He exercises at the gym three times a week, travels to Italy and France four weeks each year to be inspired for future menus. He is active on several non-profit boards primarily focused on feeding New York City's homeless and disadvantaged. He frequently walks through Central Park with his whole family, enjoying time with them. At least once a week he helps his children with their homework. His former employees now are proprietors of popular restaurants and attribute their success to the practices they learned as his employees.

CHAPTER 2

What Is Passion?

$\mathbf{D}$o you remember the feeling you would get as a kid when it was the night before your birthday or a holiday and you knew you would be getting presents the next day? Weren't you too excited to sleep? When was the last time you felt that way about anything?

You'll know the feeling I'm talking about if you are a sports fan—whether your team is the Knicks, Cowboys, Red Sox, or Notre Dame—it's that same feeling you get when the ball goes into the net (or through the goal posts or out of the park) just a split second before the final buzzer and wins the game.

If sports aren't your thing, then maybe listening to Mozart or great jazz stirs something inside of you. For me, playing tennis and going out dancing gets my blood flowing; I could do these activities for hours and still not want to stop. Yet, for someone else, dancing might be excruciating or just nothing special. Maybe you love cooking or playing chess . . .

When we are doing something we are passionate about, we feel great because we are fully experiencing the present moment and what it means to be alive. We're not watching the clock or wishing we were somewhere else because we are exactly where we want to be.

Many people live from moment to moment rather than "in the moment." They are stressed out thinking about all of the "burdens" they must endure (e.g. working, taking care of the kids, walking the dog). What's wrong with this picture? Why can't our work be fun? Shouldn't we cherish the time we have with our kids? And don't you remember how you felt when you first got that puppy?

Of course it's OK to have an occasional bad day or to feel down every now and then. But when you feel miserable (and make everyone around you miserable) most of the time, you really need to do whatever it takes to make the changes that will get you back on a positive and productive life path.

Regardless of your circumstance, there is no excuse for wasting your time, energy, and thoughts focusing on things that are negative and unproductive. That kind of thinking accomplishes nothing and chases all the good people away. Think about it. Are you attracted to people when they complain and feel sorry for themselves?

What are you waiting for? You don't need me to remind you that you are going to be dead one day. We're all going to end up as worm food (or fish food) as I like to say! That being the case, I want to use up my whole "candlewick." I want my flame to burn as big and bright as possible. Then, at the end of my life, I will be satisfied that I gave this life my all and made a difference in as many lives as I could touch. (Writing this book is one example of my personal commitment to achieve this objective.)

Once you dust off the cobwebs and start moving in a forward direction again, I guarantee you'll feel better about yourself and your life. As you begin to gain momentum, resist the temptation to take the path of least resistance. Whether it's a job, a spouse, or a house—you'll never achieve lasting happiness or contentment—if you settle and play it safe.

Let's go back to being worm food for a minute because I want you to see why living a mediocre life is not an option for anyone with the passion for success burning within.

When you see a headstone, there is always a hyphen between the dates of a person's birth and death. Why not think about that symbol as something more significant than a simple line etched on a stone? Isn't what happens during the time between these two dates what we know as "life"?

Passionate people live life to its fullest. They're not satisfied with remaining on the couch watching everything happen in black and white. I'm inviting (urging) you to get off the couch and check out what it's like to experience everything "in living color." Make your **HYPHEN ROCK!**

From now on, every time you see a hyphen, stop and ask yourself if you are proud of your life at the present moment. If you're not, then I implore you to seek out the answers you need to help you create the life you want to have.

Individuals who possess the passion for success can't wait to wake up every morning and meet the day's adventures head-on. For them, life is a game that's fun, requires strategy and skill, and is competitive. And every day the game starts over.

My golfer friends tell me on days when they are "on," they place every shot on the green, finish several strokes under par, and figure they've reached a new level of play. But the very next day (playing the very same course), it seems every ball has a mind of its own—landing in water hazards, sand traps, and up in trees!

Life is a lot like golf—it takes an entire lifetime to learn; we still can't perfect it; it's challenging (never boring); we have the opportunity to make new friends along the way; and, while we celebrate our little victories, we also agonize over those missed putts.

Every champion's greatest challenge is continual improvement—the quest to perfect the game. Most athletes enlist the help of coaches to achieve or maintain peak performance. Day in and day out, competitive athletes train with practice drills and visualization techniques, and they follow strict regimens of diet, exercise, and sleep in order to win when it is game time.

Winning in sports and life demands great discipline. Discipline without passion is tough to maintain because it requires a strong desire.

Do you desire a better life than you have now? If you don't feel passionate about your specific life goals, it will be difficult to put forth the effort required to see them to fruition.

When you are passionate about what you are doing and where you are going, how you experience time becomes altered. You feel as though you could spend endless amounts of time and still not have enough hours in the day to give to your pursuits.

If you love playing basketball, when you're out there on the court you're not thinking about the calories you're burning or that your knee hurts. Maybe, after the game, you'll remember you hurt your knee and need to ice it (but even that pain won't be intolerable because you just played a great game of basketball with your best buddies).

Our attitudes about time affect our destinies. In a single

minute some people can make decisions that literally transform their lives. Yet most people seek to "kill time"! They don't appreciate the power of the moment, and they allow minutes to fly by, wasting opportunities at every turn.

I hope you are becoming aware of a constant theme in this book: if you live in the moment, you will have an extraordinary life. When you are in the moment, it transcends time.

The primary objective of this chapter is to guide you to discover what it is that you're passionate about. Once you have identified what motivates you to get out of bed every morning, you'll want to restructure your life so that you're able to pursue that passion and experience an extraordinary life.

I absolutely believe we can make money pursuing our passions. In fact, I assert it is the only way to become wealthy. Some of us have to be more creative than others.

My parents wanted me to become a doctor. I went to Princeton University, majored in chemistry, and played for the tennis team. I loved playing tennis, but I did not have the same level of enthusiasm for a career in medicine. I thought a career in tennis as a teaching professional would be ideal for me, except (and this is a big except) I wouldn't earn the money I needed to achieve all of my life goals.

So, if I was headed for a career in medicine and my passion was tennis, how did I end up selling life insurance? Did I discover I was passionate about insurance? The answer to the second question is no. This is my answer to the first question:

A friend introduced me to the life insurance business. He told me three things about this business that appealed to me. He said, "You don't have a boss, you can earn unlimited income, and you can use tennis to develop your clientele." I thought my friend had presented an interesting way of looking at insurance sales as a career. Following our discussion, I decided to learn more about the insurance industry and sales, and I explored ways to integrate tennis into my professional life.

I earn money when I sell life insurance. I sell a lot of life insurance because I meet an extraordinary number of qualified prospects even when I'm not working. I usually meet them playing tennis!

You see, tennis is the vehicle by which I develop relationships. I am certain most of my clients would never have scheduled an appointment with me to buy life insurance if I cold-called them. Because they meet me, enjoy playing tennis with me, and get to talking about what I do for a living, if they have an insurance need they will feel comfortable to talk with me (or refer me to a family member, friend, or colleague).

So I figured out a way to pursue my passion for tennis by utilizing it as my key marketing tool. It helps me make the kind of money I want to make in order to live an extraordinary life. Think about what I am telling you. I am having fun, getting exercise, and enjoying the opportunity to get to know interesting people! You can do it, too.

Some of my golfer friends have applied this same approach to pursuing their passion for the game of golf and developing relationships that enable them to build successful businesses.

Understanding the power of networking and the basic human need to have fun, I created Life's Passions Events Planning in 1998. Our mission is bringing professionals together to pursue fun and do lots of good for different charitable causes. Over the years, we have organized a wide variety of formal and informal events.

For example, we've brought investment bankers and attorneys together at a bowling alley. When you get successful people who don't know one another onto the same team to bowl against another team of strangers just like them, you can't believe what is possible!

Status and labels (firm names, titles, salaries, and school associations) go out the window as the bowler in Lane 1 becomes known to his team as Joe. And he's competing against Bill in Lane 2. Suddenly, it's just two guys bowling against each other and getting to know each other. Before the night is out, Joe and Bill will probably exchange cards and keep each other in mind to do some business in the future. The best part of it all is that everybody initially came together to raise money for a good cause, and we all feel great because we did something good and had a fun time doing it.

I play a lot of charity tennis tournaments, and many of my

friends play in charity golf tournaments. If you make an effort to find out what is happening around you, you will learn there is an abundance of opportunities to play and make a difference and expand your network.

Imagine what can happen for you professionally (and personally) if you join an organized league for your favorite sport and see the same people week after week, sweating and competing in an activity that yields that feeling of being alive. What better way to get to know people than by doing the things you love to do and putting yourself out there? If you think you can't make the time, then you can't afford not to make the time.

Many of us hate working out, so it is especially tough to get motivated to wake up at 5:00 a.m. in order to get to the gym. The key to getting in shape is to do things you enjoy doing. Maybe you love mountain biking and hate treadmills. Maybe swimming laps at an aquatic center or jogging in the park is your thing.

If you can't get excited about any of your exercise choices, maybe you can motivate yourself by thinking how weight training and aerobic exercise will enable you to do more with your kids, friends, or coworkers.

Just recently, I was at the athletic club near my house and I was shooting baskets at 5:00 a.m. When I went upstairs for water, I met a guy about my age who was wearing a t-shirt with the name of his college and class on it. I told him that one of my biggest clients also went to his school and was in the same class. As it turned out, he didn't know him, but we talked for forty-five minutes. He ended up telling me that he is a 'wills and trusts' attorney. During the course of our conversation, I learned that he works closely with many of the Florida sales agents who represent the same life insurance company I am affiliated with in New York. We also discovered we had other mutual acquaintances. He represented one of my best friend's fathers, and he was also the former boss of another friend of mine when they worked together at the same law firm.

This morning encounter at my gym is an excellent example of how important it is to recognize the abundance of opportunities that exist all around us. In addition to the benefit of my regular routine, I met someone who told me about a basketball league I might want to join and offered to introduce me to some of the people in his network.

Some people reading this book might say, "OK, what I need to do is to make some time and learn golf." But it's not just about learning golf or bowling or tennis. You first need to spend time finding the thing about which you could become passionate. How do you find that? It takes trial and error.

Take a class in bridge or an art class. Get some travel brochures or magazines, and see what piques your interest. You must give yourself the opportunity to try out each new activity. Take a look around at the people who are in the class or on the cruise. Take a few deep breaths, and take in all the new smells (the grass on the golf course, the ocean's breeze on which you're sailing, the clay you're molding). How do you feel in this new environment? Do you think the new people around you might be the kind of people you would like to get to know?

One of the reasons I moved to Boca Raton was because I fell in love with the Old World elegance and ambiance of the Boca Raton Resort and Club. When I first arrived, something deep inside of me told me that I belonged.

What special places make you feel good and give you a sense of connection? You may need to get out of your head to recognize them. Just as in meditation, you must get centered in order to create an awareness of what feels good to you. Your best decisions are made when they come from the heart.

It's also a good idea to pay attention to your breathing. Have you ever noticed how our breathing changes depending on what we are doing? It does. When we are relaxed and content, our breathing is deep and full. If our breathing is short and shallow it's because something isn't right. It's really interesting to become aware of how our bodies react, because they often know before our minds when things are OK or not.

Remember how I described the enthusiasm of rooting for your favorite team? If a new activity or environment resonates with the same level of intensity as other things that you are most passionate about, you have found your passion. You certainly know the difference between meeting someone on a blind date who will be just a friend or who will be a love interest.

Finding your true passions requires trial and error. We follow this same process when we expose our children to new things—piano lessons, figure skating, chess, horseback riding, or soccer—and they innately recognize which extracurricular activities they love to do and which aren't for them.

So treat yourself as you treat your kids. Every day encourage yourself to try something new. Over time you will notice that you're starting to think about particular activities more than others; you want to go back and do something again and again. The things you want to go back to play again are probably in the neighborhood of your passion.

If you remember the distinction I made between rich and wealthy in the first chapter, you might be surprised that only twenty-five out of over five hundred people I interviewed fit the criteria of "wealthy." This is because in order to fit my definition of wealthy, an individual must actively participate in his or her passions.

If you are passionate about what you are doing and you are really there for the right reasons, you will become someone who attracts others. On the flip side, if you get involved in things you don't enjoy or believe in, you will be miserable and actually repel others. This is such a powerful truth that even if you pretend to like something you really don't like, your body language will betray you and people will pick up those signals loud and clear. Remember, we all come with built-in lie detectors!

When you spend time doing the things you dislike, you are abusing yourself. This is painfully evident when you are always tired, get headaches, suffer from irritable bowel syndrome, are chronically depressed . . . you name it. Recognize these symptoms of stress and address the cause to preserve your health and well-being.

Where many people err is when they find something is not working for them, yet they keep doing it over and over again, expecting a different outcome. Instead, I suggest that when you find something you are passionate about, you do it over and over again because it works for you and it gets you excited.

If you are still having trouble identifying your passions, seek out people who are clearly passionate for the things they are doing in their lives. Ask them, "What is it that has you wanting to play tennis for five hours a day?" Listen to each person's answer and look for the pattern. Then start answering this question for yourself. Once you can provide your own answer, you will know what passion feels like.

Start spending your time with other passionate people—the kinds of people who will raise you up. Create your own support structure (your Circle of Success) for finding and pursuing your life's passions.

Once you are on your way to pursuing your passions, remember to check in with your Circle of Success regularly. Your inner circle will keep you grounded and accountable. They'll tell you if you have changed or if you've lost your way.

As you will see in the next chapter, success requires passion . . . and a great deal more.

Exercises

1. Make a list of your five passions in life.
2. Participate once a week for three weeks in a passion you enjoyed in your youth.
3. Ask your three closest friends to list their top five passions in life and share them with you.

For their inspiration and guidance with the material in this chapter, many thanks go to:

Judi Bluman. For living life with boundless energy.

Betsy Spielfogel. For demonstrating a passion for children.

Bobby Green. For sharing your amazing enthusiasm in sales.

Mary McFadden. For living life consistent with your passions.

Jojo Nicholson. For inspiring everyone you train for peak fitness.

Wealthy Profile #2

Real estate developer, 60, married, living in New York City, with a seventeen-year-old daughter and a fourteen-year-old son. Runs his business out of the townhouse where he lives. His net worth is in excess of $150 million. He never works past 5:00 p.m. because he wants to spend time with his children. He goes to their country house in Connecticut on the weekends to participate in the activities his children enjoy. He enjoys collecting antiquities, playing tennis, going to Yankees games, and supporting over 100 philanthropic causes. Several of his employees say they would not have the life that they live today if it were not for his generosity and guidance. He intends to pass his business enterprise to his children and has already begun teaching them his system. When you are in his presence, you know he genuinely cares about others.

CHAPTER 3

What Is Success?

It's time to take a close look at success. One of the questions I asked the individuals interviewed for this book was, "How do you define success?"

There were significant differences in how the *rich* and *wealthy* answered my question. The rich described success via their possessions, and the wealthy defined success as the impact their lives have on others. The rich consider their possessions as accomplishments, while the wealthy regard their children and their charitable work as accomplishments.

A rich person might tell me, "I went to Harvard Business School. I'm a partner at Goldman Sachs. I have a Bentley Continental GT. I have a house in the Hamptons." Do you notice the frequent use of the pronoun "I"?

It may (or may not) surprise you to learn that the majority of the rich people were dissatisfied with their lives. They believe they'll be happy when they get what they don't have or get more of what they already have.

Every rich person had a very hard time defining his or her purpose in life. Every wealthy individual knew his/her purpose immediately, which included making a difference in the world. In fact, this is the standard of how the wealthy measure their success.

When asked what they would do differently in life, the rich responded by answering they would have gone to a different school, not had kids, or taken a job with firm X instead of firm Y. The wealthy often said they would have spent more time with their kids and taken more vacations.

All of the people interviewed for *The Passion for Success* counted the financial component of success in their definition.

And most Americans would agree that one's financial status is a measure of one's success. The key to this discussion is that material wealth is only one dimension of an individual's overall success in life.

Many people mistakenly think the entirety of life's success is tied to their net worth, their income, and their things. The fatal flaw with this belief is that once those things are taken away, or if they experience a financial downturn, their identity goes away.

For me, the true measure of success includes the quality of your relationships. Success means the people whom you met twenty years ago are still people who want to be in your life. When you have strong relationships—starting at home with your spouse and your children—you have security that no amount of money can buy.

Many of the parents I interviewed felt that a truly successful life means having a good relationship with their children—which they described as spending as much time as they could with their children, getting involved with their schools and extracurricular activities, being there to cheer them on, and being an active participant and guiding force in their lives.

Success is also the ability to envision a future and have it actualized on many different levels. I have found that success is really having the ability to attract people (family, friends, coworkers, employees, donors) and support to a vision you have set forth, and watch it come to fruition.

Success is a mindset—it's knowing that when you say something is going to happen, you're going to make it happen. You have to make your own success.

When you create your success, you have a sense of abundance because you know you can recreate that success if you lose what you have or if circumstances change. People who don't create their successes are often fearful because if they lose what they have been given, they don't know how to get it back. This is a common phenomenon among the progeny of the rich and famous.

People who don't know how to set up the practices that will

make them successful in life tend to worry a lot about not being successful. And by focusing on failure, that's what they bring into their lives.

So how do people learn how to be successful? One of the best ways is to model the successful behaviors of others. Seek individuals who have achieved success in their physical, spiritual, and/or financial domains. If it's difficult for you to find individuals who have achieved a high level of success in all three aspects of their lives, try to identify a few people who are strong in each of the different areas.

For example, if you want to improve in the area of physical fitness, recruit a friend or acquaintance willing to share knowledge and experience with attaining health, working out, and eating right. If you want to learn how to develop your spiritual self, find a role model who could teach you how to meditate or educate you about ways to do good things in the world through charity and volunteer work. And, to strengthen your financial acumen, be sure to get advice from those who have solid credit and a proven track record accumulating wealth.

What should you look for when you want to model someone's behavior? How far do you need to break it down? Do as fine an analysis as is possible and practical. For example, if you are learning about finances from a financial role model, ask for advice on how to pay your bills or save money. Ask about investment strategies. If your role model is a successful entrepreneur, learn how to create a business plan, run a business, interact with employees, and so on.

Your role model may be a friend, friend of your family, relative, prominent member of the community, or the most successful person you know. When you tell people you admire their success and want to learn how to be successful, you will find that most people will open their hearts and share their advice. They will want to help you because wealthy people want to make a difference in the world.

Here are some of the questions I ask when I interview successful people:

- What has made you successful?
- What daily habits have contributed to your success?
- If you ask your friends to describe your personality, what would they say?
- If you were going to start your business over again, what would you do? What would you do differently?
- What are some of the books I should read to set up the practices necessary for becoming a successful person?

I recommend you read *The Common Denominator of Success*, by Earl Nightingale. This book explains that successful people do what unsuccessful people are unwilling to do. This is the concept of going the extra mile. Remember the client I called every week for two years before he called me back? When I mention doing things others are unwilling to do, I do not mean doing things inconsistent with your values and your passion to achieve success. So this is a good place to address how we define success and failure.

One day you wake up and say you don't want to be a lawyer anymore. Are you a failure if you don't remain a lawyer for the rest of your working life? Well, let's answer this question with a question. If you hate what you do day in and day out, and you have identified something else you are passionate about (that would be a viable career path), wouldn't you consider yourself a failure if you didn't follow the path you have come to realize is right for you?

Chances are if you don't like your job today, you won't like it tomorrow or the next day or the day after that. Many associates get caught in the trap of thinking life will be better when they make partner. But in the first few years when they started making money, they became victims of their own success by imprisoning themselves.

They choose to rot in their jail (that is, their job) because they've invested heavily in getting where they are right now—they put in their time at the right law school, got the coveted first job with a top firm, have the impressive title and a corner office, and make an obscene salary. But at the end of the day, they haven't seen their spouse or made it home to spend time with their kids, and there is too much work at the office to take a vacation right now (or for the next few years).

If you define success by title, status, and a paycheck, then stay at the law firm. If wealth and success mean something more to you, then you've just answered the question for yourself. You are not a failure if you have grown and are a different person today than you were when you were twenty, with no real life experience, trying to decide what you wanted to do for the rest of your life.

When we are young, many of us are told that the key to our success is going to be the degree we earn, the job we get, and the money we make. While we are taught how to read and write as kids, no one actually teaches us how to be successful. Unless we were fortunate enough to have *wealthy* parents (or a mentor) we could model, we must spend our adult lives learning the secrets of success by trial and error.

I am not blaming our parents or teachers for what we don't know. Too many people spend too much time blaming others for where they are in life. I suggest you try something more effective—make the process of discovering how to achieve success a game. It's the inquiry into life that makes it exciting. If we had all the answers, the game would be over.

One of the greatest thrills we get from achievement comes from overcoming challenges and obstacles. This is where you find out what you are really made of—if that scares you, you probably should stay at the law firm.

We derive our satisfaction in life from our accomplishments. Remember, you cannot be given a successful life. You alone create your success.

As we have come to define success, it really is about creating a vision and having it realized. This vision is bigger than you and encompasses not only your life, but also the lives of those you love and those for whom you have the power to make a difference. Money is a tool to help you make your vision reality. The money you attract is not meant for you to put away where it can't circulate and serve a higher purpose. Wealthy people are successful because they know how to make money work for themselves and their causes.

Exercises

1. Interview the three most financially successful people you know. Ask them these three questions:
   a. How do you define success?
   b. What is the key to your success?
   c. How do you want to be remembered?
2. Define success for yourself.
3. Ask a child under the age of twelve to define success.

For their inspiration and guidance with the material in this chapter, many thanks go to:

Howard Cowan. For your consistently superior performance in the life insurance industry.

James O'Donnell. For not doing business with me because I was late to a meeting.

Tom Kozlowski. For sharing your expertise and your ultra-affluent clientele.

Louis Kreisberg. For showing me that the income potential in life insurance is unlimited.

Scott Efron. For overcoming adversity to triumph in the real estate business.

CHAPTER 4

Power of Team

Successful people place a high value on personal relationships.

The true measure of our individual success in life, as discussed in the last chapter, includes the quality of our relationships. So let's begin this chapter by taking stock of your current personal relationship net worth.

How do your relationships rate right now?	**Overall:**	
Spouse/significant other:	+1	−1
Children:	+1	−1
Mother:	+1	−1
Father:	+1	−1
Brother(s):	+1	−1
Sister(s):	+1	−1
Best friend(s):	+1	−1
Boss (or your Board of Directors):	+1	−1
Coworker(s) or Employees:	+1	−1
Total:		

Do you have more pluses or minuses in your relationship portfolio today? Has the overall value of your portfolio increased or decreased in the last year? Are your family relationships as strong as your work relationships?

If you regularly miss dinner with your family, cancel plans with family and friends, and can't remember the last time you spent an hour alone with one of your children, keep reading.

If your phone never rings, and the only email you get is work-related (or *spam*), keep reading.

If you feel disconnected from family and friends, that's because you are!

You may be driven to make money and to accomplish great things, but at what price? Are you willing to pay the personal cost of losing the people you love to achieve your goals?

Ready or not, here's another pop-quiz:

- Could you count on the people in your life to help you in a time of need?
- Would you be willing to do the same for them?
- If asked, would these people say they could count on you?

If you had a net worth of a billion dollars, but not a single friend, I would tell you (to your face) that while you may be rich, you are not wealthy. If you won the Nobel Prize, but no one has a good word to say about you, you are unsuccessful in life.

Note to the self-centered: there is no such thing as a self-made man (or woman). Our individual journeys to success start with a minimum contribution of food, water, and shelter from the people who raised us—our parents, grandparents, or guardians. We must also remember to count the guidance and support we received from aunts and uncles, teachers and coaches, our friends' parents, and other adults who helped shape our early lives. If any of these very important people are alive, are they still in your life?

We form our first relationships in childhood—with our brothers and sisters, cousins, classmates, and teammates. It is as children that we learn how to share, compromise, play fair, and so much more. Nothing could be simpler than this childhood advice: "To have a friend, be one." The kids who master this lesson grow up to become successful adults.

While it may seem that some of us are naturally better at developing relationships than others, I suggest we all have the same ability, but most of us get lazy. Of course every relationship takes work; everything that has value in life requires us to expend effort. That being said, there is great value in the Power of Team!

When I talk about the Power of Team, I always start by defining *power* in relation to *team*. In this context, power is the ability to move things forward. And the best way to move something forward is with the help of other people.

You can go only so far without help from anyone else. In the song, "People," Barbra Streisand sings, "People who need people are the luckiest people in the world." We all need people! Maybe the lyrics should be, "People who *realize* they need people are the luckiest people in the world." These people are very much in touch with one of life's essential secrets of success.

Once you learn to develop quality relationships with other people, your life will be extraordinary. It is only through our relationships with others that we have the ability to experience all the richness that life has to offer.

When was the last time you saw the animals in a zoo through the eyes of a small child? Would you enjoy the most romantic spot on the planet as much by yourself as you would if you were sharing it with someone you love? I rest my case!

To strengthen your personal and professional relationships, you must first strengthen yourself.

Spend some time—start with as little as one hour a week—alone. Use this time to write down the thoughts that occur to you as you clear your mind of all other distractions. During this power hour, list the victories (personal and professional) you had during the week along with some of the strengths you've noticed in yourself. Also, write down your thoughts about your future as well as some of your concerns.

You will accomplish more for your life during this single hour each week, than you will over the course of the remaining 167 hours of the week. Your power hour refocuses your energies. When you are focused and clear with your intentions, you will attract the people, tools, and resources to enable you to get from where you are now to where you want to be.

Another excellent practice for strengthening your relationships is to check in with your inner circle—your Circle of Success—every ninety days. Go to the five or six people you know (who genuinely care about you), and ask them to tell you how you are doing in your relationship with them.

Ask:

Do you feel I am always present in our relationship?

Am I acting in accordance with my values and beliefs?

Am I someone you can count on in times of need?

To realize the lasting benefit from each evaluation, you must be open to hearing the truth about yourself. Likewise, it is critical that each person be willing to tell you the whole truth (and nothing but the truth) about yourself. In the instances when they see something is not right, their constructive feedback will be more instructive for you than all the warm and fuzzy positive reinforcement you get for just doing what you should be doing in the first place.

Give each person free reign to share what they see, without interruption, and they will tell you what's really there. Some of our greatest teachers are our children because they don't edit what they say or what they see—they just go for it! You can always count on your kids to tell you what's up.

As you seek to strengthen yourself within by looking outside of yourself, remember to check in with your higher power. The relationship you have with God (please use the name you prefer) is perhaps your single most significant relationship. When you have a solid spiritual relationship you will be able to develop a clear vision of what you need to be doing with your life. Once you know where you want to go, you will attract the people who can align with that vision—and together you will make incredible things happen.

When you set goals and create a vision, you must be diligent. You will need to reevaluate each goal and vision every ninety days. This is essential for us as individuals and as people coming together to form a team in order to achieve a common objective. Whether we have a work project or a charitable event or a family goal, we have to make sure everyone on the team is still committed and working toward the same end.

Now, let's look at a few practical examples of the Power of Team. When my former business partner and I founded our financial firm, we started with just the two of us. We decided to bring our two individual practices together: his contacts, my contacts; his skill sets, my skill sets; and we agreed to split everything 50/50. Eventually we hired employees to help handle the administrative side of our business, and throughout our years working together, we checked in at least once a week to make sure everyone was reading from the same page.

In our office, we ran weekly staff meetings. In these meetings we reviewed our mission statement in order to set a context for what each member of our team needed to do. It is not acceptable to be busy without a purpose. Our work needs to make sense, and it should come from the list of action items we create to achieve each goal we set.

When our team was aligned, nothing could stop us. Everything was working because we were working together and supporting each other to produce our intended outcome.

As time went on, our Power of Team was breaking down. My partner and I grew apart, and our visions for the direction of our business and our team became different. I began to think more and more in terms of charitable work, and my partner did not share my growing passion.

We went astray once we started bringing our egos to the table. We became too caught up with who was bringing in more business (when, why, how, and with whom). We fell into the trap of focusing on who should get credit for this and that, and then our emphasis shifted from building our business together to how we should divide our monies between us.

We lost sight of our vision. We stopped working together as a team. This is certainly a common reality in life—we see it happen in marriages all the time. It takes tremendous effort to stay aligned with your teammates for the long term. We are fortunate when we can last for years or a lifetime with the same team.

In sales, the team approach is incredibly powerful. One reason it works so well is because each person brings different abilities and unique perspectives to the group. To illustrate this point using the life insurance business as an example, some salespeople are good at prospecting, others like analyzing or writing reports. We rely on employees who are very good at building relationships with customers and handling customer service, and we need skilled and experienced underwriters.

When everyone comes together and remembers to leave their egos at the door, great things can happen. When a cohesive team develops, everyone is better off (including the client) because ultimately we are happier performing our jobs. Working as part of team allows us to do what we do best, and hopefully we are doing something we are passionate about.

Sometimes we have to remember that in order to accomplish our objectives (especially in the professional leagues), we need to trade some of the players on our team or ask to be traded. We see this happen in professional sports all the time, and it's not only about the player who wants to make more money. There are times when the team just isn't working together as well as they did in the past.

When you see a team like the New England Patriots who have won the Super Bowl three out of four consecutive years, you can understand that these guys are a perfect example of outstanding, larger-than-life individual athletes who have united as a team with one common goal—winning. They understand that the team is greater than any individual player's contribution. When they forget this basic principle and let their egos onto the field, they will fail to maintain their current level of success.

Sports serve as a great metaphor for how to succeed in business on so many levels. Many former athletes (professional, college, and even high school) who come from the world of team sports bring their ability to think as part of a team with them when they enter the business world.

Individuals who attribute their success in sports to the efforts of the team, rather than their ability alone, are valuable assets to your organization. But when you meet a prospective employee who believes all success on the field (or court) is a result of his or her God-given talent, you may want to keep interviewing more candidates for your team!

Consider Lance Armstrong. This man undoubtedly has an abundance of God-given talent. He also is a disciplined athlete with a remarkable will. If you view him as an example of a great individual athlete, you are missing the bigger picture. Armstrong is the perfect model of the Power of Team. If you understand cycling, then you know that Armstrong has relied on the power of his team to help him win each Tour de France. In the sport of bicycle racing there is tremendous power generated by the "drafting" created by the riders as they race in unison.

If you have a unique ability, surround yourself with other people who have a common goal and work together (in unison) to carry each other to the finish line. This is the Power of Team incarnate.

It is truly amazing to see what we can produce when we are focused, doing what we love to do, and working in concert with a balanced team.

It is often a good idea to work with those whose styles may clash with our own (I don't mean morally or ethically). For example, I am an extrovert, and I love meeting and talking with new people. I may have a business associate on my team who is more introverted and prefers to work on financial spreadsheets with little conversation. Sure, I could view the introverted person as someone with whom I don't have much in common. And that person may find me annoying because I talk too much! But we may both be able to make significant contributions to our team.

In essence, the Power of Team is about surrounding ourselves with people who are going to help us to achieve our goals; individuals with integrity who will always be honest with us. You must take great care to be extremely selective about whom you choose to include on your team and how you spend your time together. The consequences of your decisions will impact your family, your business, and virtually all areas of your life.

While it may be painful to let go of people who have been in your life for many years, sometimes you need to remove yourself from unhealthy or negative people in order to grow and reach higher levels of self-actualization. If you have a close family member who is a toxic influence in your life, perhaps the kindest thing you can do is to decrease the amount of time you spend together. And, when you do see one another, do everything in your power to remain strong and positive.

Unfortunately, there may be some people in your life who

behave like a pot of crabs in boiling water. As the water temperature rises, the crabs that are unwilling to climb up and out of the water actually try to pull down the crabs that want to escape. People who try to pull us down lack the capacity to be happy for their successful friends or family. If you make it, then they lose their excuses for not trying harder to get what they want in life. So they have a big emotional investment in seeing you fail.

This is a common phenomenon in corporate America. Think about it. Have you ever taken initiative and found that your coworkers (or even your boss) treated you poorly instead of telling you what a great job you did? The reason is simple: you made everyone look bad because you were simply doing your job well!

Most work groups in corporate America are afflicted with serious dysfunctions: people are pulling each other down; they are not paying attention in meetings; they waste time and keep busy just for the sake of keeping busy. Far too many employees are more concerned with getting more "face time" than producing more results.

I highly recommend reading *The Five Dysfunctions of a Team* by Patrick Lencioni. It is a fable about what happens when a company's employees fail to act as a cohesive team and how they are brought back together. The book illustrates five common dysfunctional behaviors: absence of trust, fear of conflict, lack of commitment, avoidance of accountability, and inattention to results. Does this sound like anywhere you have ever worked?

Lencioni's book is incredibly valuable because it gives readers a sense of what works and what doesn't work in the form of a story. We learn that if we aren't communicating in a way that is consistent with the vision and the mission of the company, then we are doing damage to the company and ultimately to ourselves.

As technological, social, and political forces have precipitated the arrival of a new world order in terms of our global economy, it is disheartening to see that American corporations are falling farther behind their Asian competitors. One factor contributing to U.S. businesses' increasing difficulties worldwide is clearly cultural.

Asian cultures emphasize team above the individual, whereas America is the land of "free enterprise," "entrepreneurial spirit," and "rugged individualism." We are raised to put ourselves first, and often we are encouraged to blatantly disregard the other guy because he is our competitor for finite resources.

We can learn a great deal from our Asian counterparts. Asian men, women, and children respect their elders—those with experience, who have gone before them. Their cultures hold the family and the company above the individual. It is no wonder that some Asian companies were founded centuries ago. In the United States, we're hard pressed to name companies that have been in business for fifty years.

I have also noticed that many of the retired leaders of American Fortune 500 companies had military training from World War II or the Korean War. The experiences that shaped America's "Greatest Generation" gave them a greater sense of accountability, respect for discipline, and loyalty to fellow soldiers in arms than what we see in boardrooms today.

Please understand that while I laud some of America's great business leaders of past generations, I do not support the concept of the good ol' boys' network. We have come a long way as a nation as we see more women and persons of color working together in small and large businesses around the country. But we still have a long way to go. Diversity is critical to a company's ability to strengthen its foundation in order to compete in today's global economy.

As companies bring more men and women together from different races, ethnicities, educational backgrounds, etc., they will benefit from a greater pool of human resources. These people will look for new ways to stay relevant and seek insights for future innovations and for success communicating with companies in their supply chain and with consumers in the global marketplace.

Many advertising firms' creative teams bring together diverse thinkers. More financial services companies are moving toward the team approach. The model of the individual stock-broker or insurance representative can no longer compete in a world where even small investors can gain access to an entire team of financial advisors to help make complex investment decisions.

On a personal level, your experience is different from my experience. Our experiences are different from Bob's experience and Mary's experience. If our ultimate intention is to come up with a great idea that moves our product forward, moves our sales effort to a new level, and enables our company to remain competitive, we need to start thinking in terms of rounding out our teams with people who will contribute their different strengths and perspectives for all of us to share.

In case you are still wondering if you can go it alone and learn to be successful in every aspect of your life, the answer is 'no'. Do yourself a big favor and assess your strengths and weaknesses. Once you have made your list of assets and deficits, I recommend spending ninety percent of your time doing what you are best at doing—and are passionate about doing!

While many of us were taught from a young age to perfect our imperfections, I suggest this is inefficient and ultimately ineffective (especially in your work life). You will be more effective if you find others who can compensate for the areas in which you are lacking. Remember, it is important that everyone is of like mind when it comes to sharing your vision and goal.

In the world of sports, college and professional scouts make a living searching for the talent their teams need. If the team has a great defense but a weak offense, the scout may recruit a strong quarterback to be the team's next draft pick. Michael Jordan focused the majority of his effort practicing his jump shot (his best shot) even when he was at the top of his game. He didn't waste too much time working to perfect every aspect of his game, because his teammates brought their abilities to the court, too. Coach Phil Jackson's Chicago Bulls, one of the greatest basketball teams in NBA history, is a great example of utilizing the Power of Team and balance.

I encourage you to apply the Power of Team at home. Start with a vision, communicate the plan, and support one another by balancing each family member's strengths and weaknesses. You will be amazed at what your family can accomplish together. Just look at the Bush dynasty: that family has produced two Presidents and a Governor!

On a more accessible level, I have worked with many wealthy families who have dinner together as often as they can. They go away on family vacations, hold real estate as a family, and have a succession plan for their children and future generations.

These successful family teams understand the necessity of teaching their children how to model successful behavior. Often, one or both parents (or grandparents) act like coaches to teach their children about philanthropy and the value of earning an education. These individuals put their families first and put personal growth and achievement very high on the list. They understand the need to teach their children to have a purpose in life.

Exercises

1. Answer the pop quiz on page 48.
2. Ask your inner circle (three people) to answer the questions on the bottom of page 49 and the top of page 50.
3. Create a fun event for your coworkers to benefit charity. Delegate different roles and responsibilities to make it successful.

For their inspiration and guidance with the material in this chapter, many thanks go to:

Michael Kagan. For teaching me about teamwork by introducing me to the book, *The Five Dysfunctions of a Team.*

Landmark Education Team Management and Leadership Program. For teaching me humility.

Larry Brown. For befriending me and sharing your secret for consistently coaching NBA champions.

Sheri Jordan. For supporting me in completing *The Passion for Success.*

George Bardwil. For sharing the power of hiring, training, and empowering quality people to run your business so you can enjoy life.

CHAPTER 5

Finding Your Purpose in Life

Let's pretend you just won the lottery. You are the only winner, so you get the whole pot and a lump sum payout of $500 million! Now you are super-rich and never have to worry about money again. And, one more thing, you are perfectly healthy.

Once you finish shopping, decorating houses, picking out cars for family members, and return from gallivanting all over the globe, you are finally back at home and wondering what you will do today . . . and the next day . . . and the next day . . .

Can you imagine having the time and financial security to just sit and ponder what to do each day? Most likely, you are so preoccupied with the drama of your daily life and stressed from treading water in a pseudo-perpetual survival mode, that you probably don't even eat breakfast because you've got to:

   a. Take the kids to school.
   b. Catch the train to work.
   c. Count your calories.
   d. All of the above.

At 11:35 p.m. You're watching Leno or Letterman, Monday Night Football, or Nightline, and you are so exhausted that you fall asleep with the TV on again. Why are you here? (Wait! Don't answer that question just yet.)

Why are you living this day every day, year in and year out? Is it because you are doing what was expected of you? If you are married, were you expected to be married by a certain age? If you have kids, were you expected to have kids? I'll also go out on a limb and assume you live in a house (or a condo) and work for a company (or stay home with your kids) all because you are doing exactly what your parents told you to do.

At the beginning of our journey through *The Passion for Success*, I asked you if you remembered what it was like to be a kid. Do you remember what it was like to be a teenager, when you questioned everything your parents told you? At what age did you grow up and start listening to your parents?

Now, you have become your parents! If you're not already in Florida, I guess I'll be seeing you here very shortly . . . when you retire here and wait to die.

Is this really your idea of living?

Do you sincerely believe you are living your life as God (or your higher power) intended—to your fullest potential?

Do you know your purpose in life?

Sadly, in all of the years I have asked this question, only one person in one seminar was able to clearly state his purpose in life.

While many success-oriented people know how to set and achieve goals, they typically remain at that level. I meet men and women who tell me they wanted to have a home in a certain country club community and they are visibly proud when they tell me how they achieved that goal. I want to own a Bentley Continental GT, but I don't confuse this material goal with my purpose in life.

What about the children and grandchildren of the rich and famous? If they have access to everything they could ever want materially, what are their goals? To make a separate and distinct life for themselves? To attain a certain level of fame and fortune in order to be a "chip off the old block"? What are their purposes in life? (It has to be more than spending their parents' money!)

OK, let's get back to you and our lottery scenario. You now have no more worries and lots of time (and money). What are you going to do with yourself? Living an extraordinary life has to include more than having things and partying with your friends.

Once you can get to that place where you are relaxing in

your bathrobe, having a croissant and fruit by the pool, and reflecting on the meaning of your life—I want you to ask yourself how you will find your purpose in life.

You will probably need a lot of help finding the answer to this question. One very good place to start as you begin your quest for your answer is to go back to your source. I mean pray; meditate. Keep asking yourself the question, "What is my purpose?" Ask in the morning when you first wake up. Ask again at night, right before you fall asleep.

Write your question in a notebook or journal each morning and night. Then free write whatever comes into your mind without editing or worrying about spelling or sense. Just write for a minimum of five minutes. Do this exercise each day and don't stop asking, "What is my purpose?" until you find your answer.

The pursuit of your purpose and then actualizing it isn't for the faint of heart. And it isn't something you try on for only a day or a week or a year. You need to commit to getting the answer and dedicating your life to its true purpose.

Truly making a difference in the lives of others is not possible for people who are easily derailed by attending to important responsibilities in life—including taking the kids to school and going to work. Having a lasting impact on humanity requires taking the road less traveled rather than the path of least resistance.

I have noticed that wealthy people, those who are fulfilled in life, are the people who are willing to take risks. Their lives are about more than just themselves and the gathering of things, titles, awards, and accomplishments. Wealthy people understand that to have a life of meaning mandates leaving the world a better place than it was when they first arrived.

Remember the hyphen?

John Q. Smith

1964 – 2045

The hyphen signifies your life and how you have spent it. How soon will you figure out why you are here and what you are supposed to accomplish while you are alive? Most of us actually do realize our purposes, but we are discouraged by the world and fail to accomplish our primary mission.

For many of us, our purposes are the dreams we had as children. But we've been taught that our dreams are silly or impossible by our well-meaning parents, teachers, and friends. Unfortunately, they honestly believe their own words because they have been frustrated by their own failures and lack of accomplishment.

I am suggesting that young people (indeed, people of all ages) need to be encouraged to follow their dreams and nurture their passions. When we notice what moves us to tears (or we feel something resonate deep within us) and we feel compelled to take action, we have connected with our purposes.

For example, if as a young person you lost your mother to cancer, you can absolutely relate to the fact that such an experience is traumatic and terribly painful for a child to endure. As an adult, you might want to help other children as they deal with the loss of a parent.

If you have a brother or sister who is mentally or physically challenged, you have a better understanding of what it means to go through life with a disability. Since you can see the world from a different perspective than other able-bodied people, when you walk along a pathway you see it through your brother's or sister's eyes. You might want to make the path nicer for others who ride on it in a wheelchair.

As we go through our lives, messages containing answers about our purpose are continually sent our way. But because we are so caught up with the struggles of living our daily lives, we fail to receive the message.

This is one of the reasons I encourage you to make time to just breathe and meditate every day for at least fifteen minutes. If that seems too much to ask, take a break, go for a walk, and collect your thoughts. Find a method of clearing your mind every single day so you can open your psyche to receiving the messages that will help you find your purpose in life.

You also need to start paying attention. You will learn that certain things will stir you up again and again. Whenever I see a child from a disadvantaged background, I want to do something to help. I do not want that intelligent and talented child to go to bed hungry.

What moves you to the point of wanting to change what is happening?

What would inspire you to enlist others to join you in making a difference?

All too often, we are motivated to get out of our daily routines and to take action only after a tragedy strikes us personally. The late Christopher Reeve found his life's purpose only after he was in an equestrian accident and became paralyzed from the neck down. As an accomplished actor, he had reached the pinnacle of fame and fortune. He may have been rich, but he wasn't yet wealthy.

After his accident, Reeve became an activist. It was from that point on that he made his most meaningful and lasting contribution to humanity. Using his celebrity, Reeve brought much needed attention and millions of dollars to finding a cure for paralysis and to improving the quality of life for individuals living with spinal cord injury. In less than a decade, Reeve and his wife, Dana, transformed the cause he championed.

Mother Theresa had been a teacher and principal in a school for privileged children in India until the age of fifty-five, when she became a nun. During her years at the school, she was moved by the poverty and despair she saw in the world all around her. Mother Theresa discovered her purpose was to become an advocate for the world's poorest people, and she devoted the rest of her life to their cause.

What recurring themes or issues seem to catch your attention? Is there something you would like to start doing, such as helping kids, teaching the illiterate to read, or rehabilitating juvenile offenders? If none of these causes moves you to action, keep your eyes and ears open for other messages.

As the child of an interracial marriage, I have known since the age of four that I wanted to do something to bring people from diverse backgrounds together. At a very young age, I decided to be someone who would have a platform to address the issue of race and get people to examine their hearts and minds and realize that we are all God's children.

So, for me, a recurring theme is the issue of race and bringing people together. I know people are innately inclusive. Yet we use color, creed, and sexual preference as ways to distinguish and separate ourselves from each other. The point is, find a way to discover commonalities so that we can understand that we're all human beings going through life, wanting to help each other and to leave the world a better place.

This issue gets my blood going. It speaks to me on an emotional level and moves me into action. If our actions are consistent with a long-term vision that makes a difference in the world, we are on the way to experiencing an extraordinary life. Each day I ask myself, "How will I leave the world a better place twenty-four hours from now?"

I am quite fortunate because my family life was so loving and supportive. My mother, grandmother, and father taught me that I can achieve anything that I set my mind to do. In fact, my father hung an expression over our front door that we read every day:

If you think you can't, you never will.

If you say you can, at least you might.

Right?

I didn't know that I wasn't supposed to be number one in my class because I was the only Black kid in my school. That never crossed my mind. In the life insurance industry, there aren't many people of color sitting across the conference table from some of the richest and most powerful individuals in New York City.

In 1991, I got a message.

One of my financial planning clients, an African American, asked me to refer a Black trust and estates attorney to draft his will. While I had a large professional network at that time, I replied, "I don't know any." But I promised my client I would find an attorney for him.

I encountered so much difficulty trying to find a Black trust and estates attorney that I thought, *If I'm having such a hard time, I imagine others will also.* I wanted to share the message that African Americans who make it to very high levels in the professional and corporate world need to get out there and market themselves. So I created an organization called Blacks and a New Direction (BAND). Our purpose was to bring African

Americans from different professions together monthly to network.

It was awesome! People loved coming to meetings because they knew when they arrived they would meet people with like minds, who were very accomplished and positive about the future for African Americans.

Too many people mistakenly think they need to wait until they achieve a certain financial milestone or until their kids are grown before they can start focusing on their purpose in life. This is not the kind of thing you can put off. Get into the habit of regularly giving and volunteering (even when you don't have anything to give). My volunteer work is another indicator that I am on the right track in terms of my life's purpose. Volunteering literally leaves me more energized after my work is done than before I arrived.

Humans share the universal desire to make a difference and to live a life filled with meaning. Unfortunately, most adults have forgotten how to access the place in their heart that speaks to them and guides them through life. The majority of people go through life worrying about their problems and about what others are thinking.

When you focus on problems, your life will manifest problems. However, when you begin to think about where you want to go and share your purpose with people who can help you get there, you will receive everything you need to accomplish your objectives.

The Red Cross, Salvation Army, United Way, American Cancer Society, and every other benevolent non-profit organization started as one person's vision. What would have happened if the founders of these organizations believed they would never be able to accomplish anything or make a difference in peoples' lives?

If you know your life's purpose, what is stopping you from going forward to carry it out?

What if you sat down and wrote your own vision for creating a structure that would impact peoples' lives? What if you talked to others about your vision and asked them to help you?

Do you believe your purpose originates from a spiritual place? If God put you here for a specific reason, can you think of any justification for not getting started on whatever it is you are supposed to be doing?

There are so many wasted lives—people who die before ever discovering their purpose and people who die because no one reached out to help them.

So many rich people die leaving so much money behind—money that could have been used in their lifetimes to change the lives of so many less fortunate men, women, and children.

Ironically, the majority of rich people live unfulfilling lives (even in their own opinions), yet they have the power to do so much good with their time, money, and connections.

I urge you to discover your life's purpose as soon as possible. And then, I encourage you to find the people who will share your vision and make a commitment to work as part of your team to see your dream to fruition.

Remember, wealthy people are philanthropic. To make the transformation from rich to wealthy, it is not enough to know your purpose. When you become wealthy, you will be given the resources to spend the rest of your life putting your time, energy, and passion behind your cause.

I challenge you to start peeling back the layers of your life. Chances are, you knew your purpose by the age of five. It may take you some time to get to the layer where your life's dreams reside. Be patient, and be persistent. I assure you the effort will be well worth it.

I want you to remember that when you were a young kid, before anybody told you otherwise, you knew you could make a difference.

It's time to reawaken that little boy or girl inside you. Tell your childhood self that you had it right back then and now you want to bring all of your grown up experience and resources together to help you achieve the greatness you were put here to accomplish.

There are people who have been waiting a long time for your help. Don't make them wait until after you experience a tragic loss before you offer your assistance.

We all need to have a purpose in our lives in order to find fulfillment. Once you start doing good things, you'll see you want to do more and more.

Exercises

1. Write down your vision for an ideal world.
2. Every day, notice what moves you and write in your journal.
3. Interview five powerful people and ask them to share their purpose in life (e.g., your mayor, governor, president of your company, minister of the largest church or in your town).

For their inspiration and guidance with the material in this chapter, many thanks go to:

Donney Leffall. For leaving investment banking to pursue a career in the nonprofit sector after 9/11.

Scott Rubenstein. For creating East Hampton Indoor Tennis after experiencing bankruptcy.

Howard Rubenstein. For creating a powerful public relations firm through networking.

Martin Luther King, Jr. For sharing "The Dream" that inspires my life.

Beth Navon. For being the role model for those choosing to run an organization which empowers our troubled youth.

Wealthy Profile #3

Motivational speaker, 45, married with four children. Lives in San Diego, CA. He has touched millions of lives through his infomercials, workshops, and retreats. He leads an extraordinary life and is grateful for all the gifts that have been bestowed upon him by God. He encourages everyone to maximize their potential in life by taking risks, being honest, and giving back. He enjoys flying helicopters, running, exercising, and polo. He spends three months a year on an island to rejuvenate and appreciate the beauty of nature. He has overcome extreme poverty by surrounding himself with life's masters and incorporating their best practices on a daily basis. He is always looking for ways to improve himself and those around him. He has introduced some of the greatest thinkers to the world through a series of interviews on CDs, and he allows the average person to apply advanced principles in their daily lives. He is my mentor.

CHAPTER 6

Happiness vs. Contentment

What does your perfect picture look like? Is it in the frame you keep on your desk at work or next to your bed—the one with you and your true love, your two kids, and the dog? Is everyone happy and smiling, posed in front of your dream home, which is just up the path, beyond the freshly manicured lawn, protected by that white picket fence?

How does your perfect picture (whatever it is) make you feel whenever you take a good long look at it? Do you feel comforted to see yourself surrounded by the very special people who love you and enjoy being part of your team in life? Do you feel happy when you remember the moment the photograph was taken? When you stop and focus on this snapshot, are you filled with a sense of contentment? Or, no matter how perfect the picture, do you get the feeling something is missing?

Since happiness and contentment go hand in hand, the objective of this chapter is to shed light on each of these essential components for leading an extraordinary life.

If you are in the midst of your personal pursuit of happiness, first broaden your understanding of contentment. Wouldn't you agree that it is impossible to find something if you don't know what it looks or feels like?

When you look for *happiness* in a thesaurus, you will find "contentment" listed as a synonym. However, for most of us, finding happiness and contentment in daily life is not quite as easy. Consider each of the following individual synonyms for happiness and contentment. How would you fill in each of the blanks?

Happiness means: _____
Joy
Bliss
Pleasure
Nirvana
Contentment

Contentment is: _____
Happiness
Satisfaction
Peace of mind

You must be familiar with all of these basic terms, right? Aren't these questions relatively straightforward?

Yet, as I interviewed hundreds of well-educated men and women for *The Passion of Success*, I realized the majority of them couldn't define happiness and contentment in simple, concise terms. In fact, many of the interviewees who participated in this project—especially the rich—had difficulty describing these words without mentioning material things. For them, happiness and contentment are things one acquires.

No wonder many rich people are so miserable—they seek happiness in all the wrong places! Contentment is all but unattainable for them because they don't know what they're looking for.

The wealthy individuals are different. While many of these successful men and women have an innate ability to recognize their source of happiness and contentment, some arrived at their understanding of these states of being through life experience and personal evolution.

I am truly grateful to each of these wonderful people for proving to me that it is possible for all of us to find happiness and contentment. My approach to learning is to seek teachers who have attained what I want in my own life. This chapter incorporates what I have come to know with help from my friends, family, associates, and the wealthy individuals who shared their wisdom and passion for success.

There are notable differences in the levels of contentment between people from different cultures. Men and women from poorer countries are often more content than their western counterparts, and there is a simple explanation for this cultural divide. In addition to their spiritual foundation, many people from eastern cultures and Third World countries are not bombarded with the same amount of external stimuli (advertising) as we are in the West. They are not getting as many messages every day telling them that they need to buy a certain brand of gadget in order to be happy. When they come to the United States and become westernized, their levels of contentment often decrease significantly.

So, to understand the dual concepts of happiness and contentment, we will begin with a crash course in Eastern philosophy; specifically, the Eastern goal of attaining nirvana. Nirvana is similar to contentment. It is essentially an internal state of mind that Westerners would recognize as a deep, long-lasting feeling of satisfaction and peace of mind originating from within us.

Happiness seems to be more of a by-product of our external experiences—our enjoyment of our present circumstances, relationships, and things. In order to experience happiness, we are partially dependent on people and things outside of ourselves. Contentment is purely internal—achieved independent of outside influences—it can exist regardless of our external circumstances.

Most of us are striving for internal peace and contentment. But we mistakenly spend most of our time and effort chasing the people and buying the things that we think will make us happy. If our happiness depends on others and what they give us, how they treat us, what kind of raise or promotion they offer us and so on, we are dependent. And it is impossible to feel fulfilled when we are dependent.

Yet, as a society, we spend so much time, energy, and money acquiring external status symbols such as designer clothes, shoes, and haircuts, club memberships, cars, and other toys. We think that once we buy this and get that, we will live happily ever after. But, even when we succeed in filling our closets, homes, garages, gym lockers, cars, and storage units, happiness continues to elude us.

If at this point in your life you have acquired everything you could possibly want and you still aren't happy, then the time has come for you to do something radical: stop shopping. Don't make any plans to go out. Instead, stay home, put on something comfortable, and settle into your favorite chair. Tonight, stay still and chill out. Spend some quality time alone with yourself.

You will see the way to find lasting happiness and contentment is to get quiet and go within. Happiness is experienced in the present moment, and contentment is the ability to carry that happiness through from moment to moment.

Once you arrive at your destination (happiness), don't worry if you are finding it hard to make it last. By its very nature happiness is fleeting. Our goal should be to reach this state of mind as often as possible and learn the habit of being happy. When you finally experience a moment of joy, bliss, or undiluted pleasure, you will naturally want to feel it again and again. It is addictive. But, unlike drugs, happiness contributes to our health and well-being.

The pursuit of happiness and contentment is not about being lazy or never wanting for anything. On the contrary, it is about doing a lot of work to get to know ourselves and understand what our purposes are, in order to ultimately become self-actualized.

When we are happy within ourselves, we are able to be present for others—our children and other family members, employees and coworkers, and friends. But when we are unhappy, we can't pay attention to anyone but ourselves and we tend to be very ineffective in every aspect of our lives. So, as Bobby McFerrin sings, "Don't worry, be happy!"

Think about children. It's very unusual to meet a small child who worries. Children by their very nature are content. I have three-year-old twin brothers. Last summer when they were visiting me, they spent an entire hour playing with the pebbles on my driveway. That's contentment!

Did you ever watch kids at the beach and how they have such an incredible ability to amuse themselves? Just think about what they can do with sand! They love to make sand castles and bury themselves underneath mounds of it; they'll throw it and sometimes even eat it. They run and splash in the water, and at the end of the day they are both content and exhausted.

Did you ever notice how the children's parents act when they are at the beach? It's the same sunny day, the water feels great, and there are comfortable lounge chairs and lots of food and drinks for everyone. But, within minutes of arrival, the adults often start complaining: "It's too hot." "The sun is too strong." "The water is too cold." "I look fat in this bathing suit." "I hate putting on sunscreen."

What's with that? Why do we have to ruin a perfectly great day? Why would anyone want to spend time with us when we're so unhappy? What happens to people when they become adults?

What happens to us is that we lose the ability to live in the moment. When we are kids we can maintain a perfect state of contentment all day, every day. Of course, children will sometimes yell and scream and have tantrums when they want something they don't have. But until they see a new toy in front of them, they are having a great time playing with the toy of the moment.

As kids get older, they become more aware of what they don't have. They even become discontented when they can't get what they want. While this tendency serves an important purpose, which is to cause every human being to strive for a better life, society has taken things too far. What does it say about our culture that as kids we learn the expression, "The grass is always greener on the other side"?

The logic to chasing the proverbial carrot on a stick is that everyone needs continual motivation in order to grow in life. A common flaw in our thinking is that we can only be motivated by external rewards—money and more money! So, once we achieve the goal (e.g., make a million dollars), we need to make a new goal because otherwise the game is over. So now the goal becomes making two million dollars.

Are you starting to see the dynamics at play? If we don't keep the game moving forward, we will find ourselves at a standstill. Then we fear we may fall behind or actually start going backwards. This will not happen if you choose to take your game inside. In fact, if you begin playing the internal version of the game, you will never get bored! It's kind of like the video games your kids play—you'll keep reaching new (and more challenging) levels of play, and you'll want to keep playing.

Before continuing, I want to clarify my position on "things." I appreciate fine cars, homes, and toys, and I will sometimes refer to them when speaking of my own personal financial success. But I own my things—they don't own me. The question I have for you is:

Do you have the things, or do the things have you?

Let's say you have four homes in different countries around the world. Someone has to take care of each home, so you may have a staff to maintain each property. You need all sorts of insurance on each home, and you probably should visit all four houses from time to time.

In 2004, homes in Florida and on many of the Caribbean islands (the Bahamas, Jamaica, and Bermuda) were damaged and even destroyed by the season's onslaught of hurricanes. One of my clients lost homes in Palm Beach and the Bahamas and even a plane.

When you worry about your net worth to the point that you have gobs of insurance, but you still lie awake at night fearful that you might lose everything, your things own you.

However, when you are truly content, you will be able to handle adversity much better than someone who is very insecure and reliant on possessions. So, while one person may fall apart when a hurricane washes away everything, another person may respond with a great deal of inner strength—and build a bigger, stronger house.

It's not bad to have a big home or to achieve success. It is important for our happiness that we maintain a healthy balance when we set out to acquire material things in life. We need to ask ourselves why we actually want the bigger car. Is it because we want to show our neighbors that we are more successful, or do we need a vehicle with more room so our family and friends will be more comfortable and safer?

We also must remind ourselves why we are working all the

hours we are working. Is it because we need to make more money in order to buy more things so we can impress everyone we know? Or are we working long hours because we are satisfied by what we do?

I meet many corporate executives who are not content with their lives, even though they have achieved high levels of professional success. Their discontent comes from their personal sacrifices; consequently, they've missed time with their families or compromised their values and sometimes their integrity. It is difficult to be content when you aren't proud of yourself.

In contrast, wealthy executives, entrepreneurs, and other high achievers who are happy and content do something most people fail to do. They maintain their connections with the people who mean the most to them in their lives. And they make sure to check in with their family members, friends, and coworkers to stay on track and maintain a balanced life. They also listen to the feedback they get and integrate what they hear into their daily lives.

Many successful people hire therapists or business coaches to help them stay grounded. Whether it's a trusted friend or a licensed professional, you need to elicit and heed the advice of people who are looking out for what is best for you.

If someone close to you tells you to relax, take a deep breath—resist any urges to bite any heads off! Chances are you will be happier if you take the well-intentioned advice.

Maybe you've been stressed out and no amount of looking inward is going to make you happy right now. If that's the case, take some time away from the office. Head off to a family vacation or a personal retreat. Maybe you need to go backpacking or reconnect with your kids for an afternoon.

Do this exercise with your kids: From time to time, ask your kids to give you an honest evaluation of how you are doing as a parent. Kids are unbelievably honest. In addition to giving you the facts as they see it, they'll go one better—if your breath stinks, they'll tell you!

We all need this kind of honesty in our lives. It keeps us real and it gives us the opportunity to make choices that will lead to greater happiness and contentment.

I also recommend checking in with your spouse, employees, or coworkers. They'll probably sugarcoat their feedback more than your kids, but their observations and recommendations will still be invaluable. We all need to learn what we can do better so we can make necessary changes and take actions that will enable us to grow.

Here are a few questions you can ask when you check in with your kids and the four or five people closest to you:

- What is it that you like about me?
- What don't you like about me right now?
- Has anything I've done disappointed you? If so, why?

I meet many people who begin to make changes in their lives—wanting to reconnect with family and friends—only after a health scare or personal tragedy. But sometimes I come across people who are smart enough to start making changes to their lives early on. These individuals want to be happy and content; and they want to experience all that life has to offer.

If you are reading this book, you are probably at least willing to try some of my suggestions on for size. But please don't think I am suggesting that only my way works. I am simply sharing what has worked for me and others I've met. Maybe some of these ideas will be right for you. Then again, maybe some won't. But you won't know what might work until you try it out for yourself. What do you have to lose?

You can absolutely transform yourself from miserable to happy and content. Remember Scrooge, the mean old man in Charles Dickens' novel, *A Christmas Carol*? Like Ebenezer, once you open your eyes and let the people around you show you the impact you have had on their lives (remember to ask for the unedited version—you want the good, the bad, and the ugly), you will see yourself in a new light.

One of the best indicators that you are on the right track in life is to look to your children and see whether or not they are successful in their own lives. If you don't like what you see and believe their behavior is modeled after your own, you can change how you live your life.

It may take a lot of work and even a few years to turn things around, but once people see you are making a sincere effort to become a better person, you will be amazed by how much love and support you'll receive as you make the necessary adjustments to how you live your life.

As long as you are moving forward, your power of team will help you with your progress every step of the way. And, as you begin to seek happiness and contentment through personal growth and reconnection to the most important people in your life, you will actually feel a new, lasting sense of happiness and contentment.

Exercises

1. Ask your children the questions on page 76.
2. Each day, write down one thing for which you are grateful.
3. Intentionally smile ten times a day for no apparent reason.

For their inspiration and guidance with the material in this chapter, many thanks go to:

Kathleen Bernard. For sharing your warm, enthusiastic personality on the tennis court.

Sara Varona. For teaching yoga and massaging me with your peaceful energy.

Sarah (my Grandmother's housekeeper). For being the love force in my grandmother's home.

John Holland. For being a humble, talented athlete and tennis partner.

Richard Schneider. For teaching me how to laugh and enjoy meeting new people.

Wealthy Profile #4

Money manager, 42, married, with a twelve-year-old son and a seven-year-old daughter. Lives in New York City. His grandfather was a very successful money manager who decided the common practice of leaving your entire fortune to your children and grandchildren creates a sense of complacency. He encouraged his children to develop their own businesses using the strategies and techniques they learned from him. Most of his childhood friends live off their own family's fortune and are not leading productive lives. He is very active with charitable pursuits that provide a head start to inner-city children. He spends almost every weekend at his country house in upstate New York, playing tennis, fishing, and reading. He is known to his employees as an extremely humble, kind boss who genuinely wants to see them lead fulfilling lives.

CHAPTER 7

Focus

As we continue our analysis of the mindset of life's consummate champions, the ability to focus stands out as another highly developed personality trait common among the most successful individuals who were interviewed for *The Passion for Success*.

Starting every day with a clearly defined intention and pathway will give you a significant edge as you endeavor to lead a more meaningful, productive, and richer quality life. But, be forewarned, you may find focus to be the most challenging skill to cultivate because it demands extraordinary levels of concentration and discipline.

At the risk of sounding like a broken record (or scratched CD), I suggest that you begin the daily practice of meditation for fifteen to twenty minutes at a minimum. Meditating allows you to clear your slate and let go of the worries, problems, and other issues preventing you from focusing all of your energies on the endeavors that will ultimately lead to the accomplishment of your goals.

Since the power of intention is so powerful, let me caution you to be mindful of your thoughts. When you focus on obstacles and excuses rather than solutions, you will fail to see the answers you need (even when they are right in front of you). Keep in mind that it is also a tremendous drain on your brain to spend time worrying. Someone once said, "What worries you, masters you."

Remember to keep focused on where you want to go, and surround yourself with people who are aligned with your vision. It is especially helpful to find friends and teachers who are willing to call you on the carpet when they see you getting off track, losing sight of your vision, and falling back into negative thought patterns and behaviors.

It is helpful to learn from the mistakes of others. Looking back at my own life, I was extremely focused for the first eighteen years. My focus was on being perfect—whether that meant being the perfect son, brother, friend, or student. But the problem with this thinking is that humans are innately imperfect. I was setting myself up for failure every day because I focused on achieving the impossible. I did not have healthy, balanced, and realistic objectives.

There are many examples of people who have reached the pinnacle of success in one area of their life through sheer willpower and focus. But these same successful athletes, entrepreneurs, scientists, and others like them, often focus too narrowly on one goal or area of life—such as their careers—at the expense of everything and everyone else.

Of the 513 men and women I spoke with whom each had an estimated net worth exceeding $10 million, 95 percent worried about not having enough or losing their money. And, while they had plenty of money (because they were so focused on having money), their personal lives were a mess because they failed to focus on their loved ones, friends, health, and other positive aspects of life. Many admitted to struggles with alcohol, drugs, obesity, and depression.

It is certainly possible to focus on more than one goal and be successful. You may be the type of individual who prefers to successfully achieve one goal before focusing on a new goal. Or you may be comfortable with shifting your focus where and when it's needed as you set out to accomplish numerous goals.

Even Olympic champions must start out focusing on winning their very first events on the fields at school. As these athletes progress, they must continually refocus on the next event and a new record.

After winning Olympic gold, many young athletes see their whole lives in front of them. Rather than resting on their laurels, they set their sights on careers (perhaps starting with professional sports), family, and the pursuit of other life goals. They know what it takes to succeed, and they simply apply the same discipline and laser beam focus to help them realize their full potential in other rewarding areas of their lives.

Let's take a moment to examine focus on the micro and macro levels. When I play tennis, I step onto the court with the goal of winning the match (macro level). However, as I play each point, I must concentrate on a sequence of present moments—my serve, then my opponent's return, then my cross-court shot. This is focus on the micro level.

When I lose a point, I cannot afford to waste my mental concentration on the lost point because now it's history. I must continually refocus on the present and play each point, giving it my all. Although I begin with the end in mind, I focus on the moment and what it will take to execute the play successfully, so that ultimately I will have more wins than losses (especially on the points that matter) in order to be the victor at the end of the match.

If you are a champion in one area of your life, then you already have the ability to focus. I'm suggesting that you take this potent power and apply it to other dimensions of your life that matter—such as raising your children or nurturing your grandchildren.

I want you to consider the importance of being present—fully focused on each moment. If you are with your children, focus on them. When you have your cell phone on one ear or your television turned on, you may be physically present in the same room as your kids, but you are not mentally present. You must be physically, mentally, and spiritually present in your relationships if you want them to succeed.

I challenge you to rid yourself of all distractions and really be with your children. If you want to have a fulfilling relationship with each of your children when they become adults, you need to focus on how you play each point now. If you wouldn't talk on your cell phone when you are trying to make that birdie on the golf course, why would you allow such a distraction to occur when you are playing with your kids?

Now let's turn our focus to the office. To have successful relationships with your employees or coworkers, you need to focus your time, attention, and energy on building those relationships. No matter how talented a doctor, lawyer, financial wizard, or CEO you may be, your success ultimately requires the cooperation of a team of people.

So, when someone walks into your office to help you finish a contract or sales presentation, you need to shift your focus from your computer screen to the person who has come to help you get the job done.

If the goal is to close the deal and earn the money associated with it, don't lose sight of the most important person—your client. Be sure your presentation communicates the value of what you will provide to your client in exchange for the money you hope to earn. If you fail to focus on showing your prospects how you will take care of their needs (because you are only focused on your commission check), then you won't make the sale or the money.

Focus on people not just things, accolades, and money. Regardless of what you do for a living, making money cannot be your only focus. Money is an outcome; it should not be your sole goal.

If you have succeeded on the financial side of your life, then you already have proof that you can succeed wherever you put your focus. I urge you to shift your focus where it's needed to achieve a healthy balanced life. Apply your powers of determination to becoming a better parent; physically fit and healthy; and, reconnecting with your Source (the juice that runs your battery).

If you have spent twenty-five years focusing on making money and ignoring your physical health, spiritual well-being, and relationships, you will probably need some support redirecting your energies and repairing those muscles that have atrophied from neglect. Engage the power of team and your Circle of Success, or seek help from a personal coach, therapist, clergyman, rabbi, or business coach. Let the people you trust guide you with constructive advice and feedback as you begin working on strengthening all parts of your life.

I am willing to bet that by virtue of the fact that you are reading *The Passion for Success*, you are a "type A" personality. You want to win at everything, and you want an extraordinary life. So let's see how you score on this Total Life Success questionnaire. It is composed of sixty questions designed to help you assess where you rank today in the three main realms of your life: physical, financial, and spiritual.

Financial Self-Assessment

1. What percentage of your gross income do you save?
2. What is your net worth?
3. How much do you have in liquid assets?
4. What are the terms of your mortgage(s)?
5. What monthly income do you want at retirement?
6. Do you have valid, executed wills?
7. How much life insurance do you own? What type?
8. What is your risk tolerance (on a scale of 1-10)?
9. What is you greatest financial concern?
10. How do you define financial security?
11. Do you rent or own your home/apartment?
12. What is your outstanding debt?
13. What are your monthly expenses?
14. Whom do you consult when making financial decisions?
15. How wealthy do you want to be?
16. At what age do you realistically want to retire?
17. Who are the three richest people you know well?
18. How long could you survive if you became disabled?
19. What would you do if you won a $250 million lottery?
20. What one thing would you like to change about your financial self?

Physical Self-Assessment

1. How often do you exercise?
2. What is your percentage of body fat?
3. What medications and/or drugs do you take?
4. How many alcoholic beverages do you consume per week?
5. What is your blood pressure?

6. How many calories do you consume per day?
7. When you look in the mirror without clothes, how do you feel?
8. How often do you have sex/ make love?
9. How often do you have a full physical checkup?
10. What are your greatest physical challenges?
11. How many hours per night do you sleep?
12. What is your greatest physical achievement?
13. How many hours per week do you watch TV, DVDs, or surf unproductively online?
14. How often do you eat red meat (beef, veal, lamb, etc.)?
15. How often do you eat sweets (desserts, muffins, donuts, candy, etc.)?
16. What is your height and weight?
17. What would you like to change about your body?
18. What vitamins and/or dietary supplements do you take?
19. How much water do you drink each day?

Spiritual Self-Assessment

1. How often do you pray?
2. How do you demonstrate your belief in a higher power?
3. What percentage of your annual income do you donate to charity?
4. How often are you moved to tears?
5. What was your most recent good deed?
6. Do you consider yourself a good listener?
7. How much time do you spend with your family each week?
8. What is the greatest emotional challenge you face?
9. Who are your idols and why?
10. For what do you want to be remembered?
11. What charitable organizations do you support with time and/or money?
12. How many close friends do you have? Who are they and why are they friends?

13. What regular religious practices do you follow?
14. What gives you the greatest joy and satisfaction?
15. How often do you smile and/or laugh?
16. What self-development workshops have you completed?
17. How much do you love yourself (on a scale of 1-100)?
18. What is you greatest fear?
19. What are the key factors when choosing a romantic partner?
20. What do you provide to the people in your inner circle?

Use your answers to the Total Life Success questionnaire to guide your understanding of what aspects of your life would benefit from a more focused effort on your part. Just as we review our financial portfolios at regular intervals, it's a good idea to review our Life Plan Portfolios every ninety days. Reallocate your attention to the areas you have neglected. Then challenge yourself to regain your balance in less time after your next Life Plan Portfolio review.

At the onset of this chapter, we reviewed the value of starting each day with a clean slate and having clearly defined intentions. We also laid the groundwork for how to achieve success by adapting our ability to focus and extending this aptitude to all aspects of our lives. Now the time has come to start behaving like you are serious about being successful.

How can you set out on your road to success if you don't know where you want to go? Whether you define your next success as making partner in your firm, giving your child an Ivy League education, or lowering your cholesterol, write it down.

Less than one percent of the population sets goals. It is estimated that a very small percentage of people write down their goals and share their intentions with people who will hold them accountable. But it is this minority who attain the highest levels of success in our society.

If you have a sincere desire to join the extraordinary life club, you need to go the extra mile to do what it takes to succeed. You may only need to make slight adjustments to your current behaviors to realize significant life gains—so, just do it! Humor me. Write it down.

Tony Gordon is one of the most successful people in the life insurance business. This impressive Englishman has earned over a million dollars a year for more than a quarter of a century. He attributes his success to his ability to focus on achieving his daily goals. Each morning he sets out to accomplish his written goals for the day. If he doesn't achieve all that he set out to do, he stays until he gets it done. Some days, Tony is able to leave at 2:00 p.m., but there are days when he may be at his desk until 2:00 a.m.

Tony also tracks his results. Speaking at a recent life insurance conference, Tony told his audience that 18.1 percent of the people he met did not have a second meeting with him. But he closed 67.3 percent of the insurance deals with people who went to a second meeting with him.

Successful people like Tony know exactly how many calls they have to make to schedule enough appointments, make enough presentations, close enough sales, earn enough commissions, and reach specific monetary goals.

But it simply isn't enough to have goals. You must write them down in order to measure your progress and track your success. You need to review your goals every day. Most people who write goals, do so once a year (usually around New Year's Day) and take the list out when it's time to write goals for the next year. What's the point of that exercise?

Taking my cue from the life masters who shared their secrets of success with me, I now set daily goals and write the associated actions required to accomplish each goal. The reason it is important to write goals down and review them daily, weekly, monthly, quarterly, and annually, is so we can use them as our life's "to do" list and keep ourselves on track. Making the extra effort to write everything down has made a remarkable difference in my rate of success.

Breaking each goal down into action steps also enables us to reach our destination (no matter the distance) by following our mini road map one step at a time. Have you ever heard the question, "How do you eat an elephant?" One bite at a time.

I have introduced the practice of goal setting to my work team. It helps everyone to focus and stay in alignment. One of the reasons corporations and many non-profit organizations have written mission statements is to keep employees focused on the bigger goal as they work on mundane tasks.

For example, if the mission of a cancer research program is to find a cure for cancer, the organization may need to send out a direct mail campaign appealing to potential donors for financial contributions to underwrite the cost of the research. While the written goal of the organization may be "to find a cure for cancer," one action step would be stamping envelopes for the fundraising campaign.

I recently incorporated another simple practice I learned at a workshop entitled, "The Seven-Day Focus." The premise of what we were taught at the seminar is to focus your efforts and energies on the actions that will yield the greatest return. Every day make a list of all the things you want to accomplish, and then prioritize your list. Next identify the top three activities with the greatest payoff potential. As an insurance professional, I must focus my time and energy on prospecting, getting referrals, and face-to-face meetings each day.

In the insurance business, a Million Dollar Round-Table Producer typically earns $70,000 in first-year commissions. On average, a Million Dollar Round-Table Producer goes on five new sales appointments each week. A Top-of-the-Table Producer goes on ten new sales appointments each week, which represents exactly double the amount of activity of the million-dollar producer. However, the Top-of-the-Table Producer will earn roughly $400,000 in first-year commissions, nearly six times the income for only twice as much work!

Most CEOs spend only seventeen percent of their time on the activities that have the greatest impact on their companies' bottom lines. Imagine how much more profitable and productive their corporations would be if they focused on increasing this percentage by just a few percentage points.

These are tangible examples of why it is so important to

focus on producing results each and every day. We can also see how critical it is to track our results, so we have a daily feedback mechanism to measure our progress toward our goals.

We often get lost in what we are doing and forget why we started doing it in the first place. But if we remember that we are licking stamps because we are giving our time to help find a cure for cancer, this activity has infinitely more meaning than simply licking stamps.

This basic truth applies to all areas of our lives. When we remember to focus on why we are working—to afford a safe, comfortable house for our family, to give our children the best education possible, to create a better life—we see our work as serving a greater purpose.

So, keep your eye on the ball, stay focused, and start getting more from this game of life!

Exercises

1. Make a list of three different things you will accomplish every day for two weeks. Share the list with a member of your inner circle. At the end of each day, report on your completion.
2. Find a quiet place and focus on a spot for five minutes. Notice your emotional state during the process.
3. Write down your top three concerns in life. Focus daily on the solution to those concerns.

For their inspiration and guidance with the material in this chapter, many thanks go to:

Tony Gordon. For your consistent "Top of the Table" production while giving back to the insurance industry.

David Grain. For showing me the habits which consistently produce outstanding results.

Steven Panagos. For being one of the core advisors for my entrepreneurial ventures.

Daniel Gregory. For allowing me to see the results of persistence.

Vince D'Addona. For being a brilliant life insurance advisor for very complex matters.

Wealthy Profile #5

Philanthropist, 41, married, with three-year-old twin girls. Lives in Westchester County, NY. She is the granddaughter of the founder of a prominent Wall Street firm. She has dedicated her life to making the world a better place, particularly in the area of empowering young women. She sits on several non-profit boards and encourages her friends to give back by having fundraisers at her home for her causes. She has boundless energy and a magnetic personality. She loves dogs, exercising, and hunting. She married for love, even though it would have been more acceptable to marry another privileged individual. She was the godmother of an HIV positive African-American teenage girl for six years, until the girl unfortunately passed away. She spent a minimum of five hours per week mentoring, encouraging, and supporting her goddaughter through her physical, emotional and financial challenges.

CHAPTER 8

Dancing with Life

Relationship—what comes to mind when you hear someone utter this word? Do you experience good feelings or a moderate-to-severe stress reaction?

If you consider yourself someone who is "good at relationships," qualify that—are you good at *all* relationships or just some?

Dancing with life is about relating. In this chapter we reevaluate the quality of our relationships with our dance partners, who include:

- our intimate partner,
- members of our immediate family,
- friends,
- coworkers and other business associates,
- tennis partners or fellow club members,
- clients, and
- everyone else we meet on the dance floor of life.

Every time we step into a room with someone, we are actually stepping onto a dance floor. Maybe you thought dance floors only exist in nightclubs and catering halls, but there are dance floors at home, at the office, in the grocery store, and outdoors.

At rush hour, the city sidewalk becomes a jam-packed dance floor. Individuals become part of the crowd and form a disjointed dance—passing, pushing, avoiding, hurrying, strolling, running, and rollerblading—all moving forward, but on very different wavelengths.

I love to tell people in my seminar classes to go play in the traffic the very next time they cross a city street after work. I tell them to stop, look, and smile. Try it. You'll be amazed to see what happens next.

First, notice how people don't look at each other. Then, look the people in the oncoming lane of pedestrian traffic right in the eye. And smile!

Your behavior will break the pattern of the people who come in contact with you. Typically, a stranger will think you look familiar and will smile back.

You can literally stop a whole lane of pedestrian traffic because when you connect with even one person, you change the rhythm of everyone else. You'll shake things up by shifting the collective energy. This is just one manifestation of the ripple effect—how our actions impact everyone around us.

In that moment when you get someone to focus on your smile, you've redirected his (or her) thoughts away from worrying about catching the train, a lost deal, and what to eat for dinner. You've caused that person to get out of himself. He may think about your smile for just a split-second or for the rest of the day.

If you regard this exercise as silly, you are missing a core message of this book. To master life, you need to stop taking yourself so seriously. Life is beautiful! And, as I will keep repeating, life is a gift we are all given to enjoy and experience in all its richness.

You may need to turn up your transmitter so you can start receiving all of the powerful messages that come out of every moment of every day. You've got to hear the music, feel the rhythms, and learn how to dance with life.

When will you decide to resonate with the universe in such a way that you are fully aware of what's going on around you?

You don't want to remain the person at the party who doesn't know how to dance—so self-conscious, uptight, and worried about how you look that you can't let go, enjoy the music, and follow it where it takes you. So, as your self-appointed dance instructor, I have enrolled you in The David Roy Eaton School of Dance!

Now, getting back to the present, my goal is to motivate you to lighten up, put on your dancin' shoes, and start having fun. I want to teach you how to cha-cha and salsa your way across every dance floor in every room you enter.

It's not enough to go through life only knowing one dance. Sometimes the band plays hip hop, other times you'll hear the merengue or rock 'n' roll. You may need to get in step for a lively line dance or a staid waltz. So, let's add some new steps to your repertoire!

When was the last time you listened to a different radio station or put a fresh CD into your sound system? Can you recall the last time you jammed to the music as loud as you could play it (in the car, in the shower, or at a party with your friends)? No matter how long ago that was, I'll bet you still remember how much fun you had and how good it felt to let yourself go where the music took you.

When you are able to dance in life and are a confident lead, you will attract many dance partners. You must also understand how to dance your partner's dance. I can dance with any woman in the room because I become aware of my partner, the rhythms of the music, and the steps.

When I dance, I focus on the pacing, breathing, and movement of my partner in order to get in sync. Once I get in step with my partner, I judge how close to move in. I observe and mirror my partner before attempting to take control by changing her speed or the flow and our proximity.

This is identical to the dynamics of establishing rapport with clients during the sales process. In sales, just as in dancing, there are lots of guys who go for it, move in too close, too soon, and cause the dance partner to withdraw—I see it happen in business deals all the time.

If it didn't cost the company money, we could just laugh at how comical it is to watch a klutz blow a big sales presentation. I'm talking about the dork who steps out onto the boardroom dance floor without taking time to observe his prospective dance partner (the client). This is the dude who steps on everyone's toes, needs breath mints, and only knows The Hustle!

Relating well to others is essential to our ability to develop successful relationships. And clearly, meaningful relationships are vital to leading an extraordinary life. If you've been dancing to the beat of your own drummer for too long, you may have forgotten how to dance with others.

Let's give you the benefit of the doubt and assume you have exceptional social (and dancing) skills. Perhaps you must deal with a difficult client—someone with a screaming "type A" personality—who is a loud, obnoxious know-it-all. How would you go about building a relationship with such an individual?

Rather than stepping onto the dance floor together, you might prefer to step out onto a mat. When you face a tough opponent like that, don't back down. Try applying some good old-fashioned martial arts instincts to the situation. Redirect your opponent's aggression back onto himself.

Think back to how you may have handled business adversaries during a tough negotiation. How did it go?

- Did you find a solution that enabled you to succeed?
- What could you have done differently?
- Did you take time to observe your partner?
- Did you know the dance steps?
- Did you establish rapport before attempting to take control of the discussion?

As we build rapport, it is critical to spend time on our adversaries' side of the table and look at the dance floor from their perspective. Put on their dancing shoes and spend some time walking around in them.

When we want someone to dance with us, it is necessary to appreciate where they're coming from. When we put ourselves in another person's shoes, we gain a greater insight into how they feel. We may even start to feel the same way they do about the issue we're debating.

This is how we get in sync and form a "meeting of minds." Once you establish (and acknowledge) your common ground on the dance floor, you can change the dance and move forward together almost effortlessly.

To learn what frequency my prospective dance partner (client) is tuned into, I will ask questions that even their friends aren't comfortable asking. I ask because I want to know more about my clients. I want to try dancing in their shoes.

In my business, people tell me everything about their money, even details I'd rather not know. The reason I am so successful at having people open up to me is that I am interested in learning about them and I care about them. And they know that I love hearing their stories.

However, when people are not genuinely interested in their prospective dance partner, it's totally obvious. Many people treat the person they are dating or the client they are courting like a trophy they want to show off. When they get out on the dance floor together, you can see how nothing flows. Everything is forced, even their smiles.

You can't fake authenticity when it comes to relating to people. If you aren't real with people, they will have their guard up. And, if you are a selfish, self-absorbed dance partner, you can forget about asking for the next dance.

At your company's next holiday party, or at the next family event, get a good spot at the edge of the dance floor. Watch all of the dancers. Keep an eye out for the people who are very stiff as they dance. These are the individuals you must be cautious with in the corporate environment and in your personal life because they are not comfortable with themselves. Unfortunately, when people are filled with insecurity they often hurt other people as they try to make up for their own deficiencies.

Sometimes, those awkward dancers don't have a hidden agenda. They're still trying to find the music that makes their souls sing. At the beginning of an old Steve Martin movie, *The Jerk*, Martin's character is listening to the radio. He is a white man who was adopted by a black family (but he doesn't know that he was adopted). He can't dance like his brothers and sisters because he has no rhythm. (Don't you love these stereotypes?) One day when no one is home, Martin changes the radio to another station and hears Frank Sinatra for the first time. Suddenly, he can dance!

There are many people who are tuned into the wrong radio station, and they need to adjust the dial to pick up something different. There is a whole world of music out there—symphonies, concertos, jazz, blues, show tunes, gospel—something for everyone.

We must all find our own dance. Take time, dwell on your dreams, and find your life's music. Dance the dance that is in your soul.

Start with your passion. Don't waste your precious time doing things that don't provide you with any sense of fulfillment, enjoyment, or connection. If you take up golf because you've been told it's a great way to build your business, but you'd rather be playing softball, you won't be good at golf. You'll look like the dancer with two left feet every time you step onto the green.

If your true love is country-western music, do yourself (and your dance partners) a favor, don't pretend to love Latin dancing! Be who you are, embrace your style and swing your partner.

People want to dance with others who enjoy dancing the same dances, and people like to work with people who enjoy the same work. If you are passionate about finding a cure for Alzheimer's or cancer, seek out others who are on the same wavelength. People will be drawn to you when they sense that your lives and missions are in harmony.

Before you start dancing with your partners, be sure to communicate what dance you'll be doing when the music starts. If you are making a team presentation for work or a fundraising appeal, choreograph and rehearse everything.

Choreography in business is equivalent to establishing an agenda and deciding who will present first, how long each person will talk, where you should stand, what each individual will say, who will lead, and so on. It's even a good idea to discuss "costumes"—when everyone on your team wears the same color suit, you'll look more uniform and professional.

I cannot emphasize strongly enough the benefit of learning to speak with one voice. This is critical for work teams of every size in both corporate America and the not-for-profit world. There cannot be one note of discord because your audience will catch it. It is not sufficient to share a vision or a mission. Each member of the group must learn his or her steps, come to rehearsals, and get aligned with the entire corps. You cannot show up on the day of the big presentation and hope everyone has studied the music. You've got to spend time dancing together in order to become one.

Group dancing is very popular and common to most cultures. You've probably linked pinkies with others at a wedding or two over the years. You know what I'm talking about—when your aunt pulls you out of your seat and over to the dance floor, you form a circle with everyone else, and you kick your right foot, then your left foot; get led to your right, and then everyone forms a Conga line and dances their way by every table. Chairs get knocked over, and you get pulled in different directions. This is amateur hour at its finest moment!

However, when you go to the ballet or see the Rockettes at Radio City Music Hall, you see what is possible with training and practice. Each dancer works for hours, day in and day out, to perfect the dance. And all the dancers come together to rehearse as a unified dance troupe.

It isn't enough to practice your own steps by yourself. All teams must spend time developing together in order to perform successfully as a single unit. This holds true on the ball field, in the office, and at home.

Successful families have mastered the art of communicating with each other. These families understand how to balance the needs of the family and support each individual. When you meet a family whose members are in harmony with one another, you will soon learn about its power. This omnipotent spiritual bond transcends individual achievements, titles, and wealth.

Great families often have a great patriarch or matriarch or both. Who is the leader in your family? Do you have what it takes to carry the next generation forward?

Family leaders have vision. They are inspiring coaches, gifted choreographers, and self-confident individuals who communicate openly and honestly with conviction.

If you are going to lead the dance, you must know the steps cold. When you are teaching your children how to dance with life, you have to be at the rehearsals and patiently teach everyone the steps. This is loving leadership. And it is beautiful to watch a family who enjoys dancing together.

How do you dance with your kids? Kids are formidable dancers because they are really connected to their music and how they want to express themselves. When you dance with your children, the key is to be a strong lead and support them as they perform their solo dances and learn to dance as one with the family.

Somewhere along the way countless families have lost the balance of power. I often see spoiled kids from affluent families telling their parents what to do! Who is leading whom? Too many parents today are uncomfortable disciplining their kids, but discipline is necessary to teach children how to succeed as adults. Isn't the ultimate goal of parenting to raise healthy, well-adjusted, socially responsible adults?

How can we influence our children if we don't spend quality time together every day? In the old days, families sat around one radio or one black-and-white television set to listen to the same family programs. Now, everyone is isolated in their individual room, watching their favorite cable TV show or surfing the Internet or listening to their iPods!

When I was a kid, my family watched Ed Sullivan on Sunday nights together. We shared our downtime together. We talked about the show's guests. We sat in our favorite chairs in the same room and actually interacted with each other.

Don't stop at asking yourself what happened to those days. If you want to win the grand prize in the dance contest of life, you'll need to coax everyone in your family out onto the dance floor.

Initially, don't offer anyone choices about what music everyone wants to listen to. You pick the song (or the activity). Maybe tonight's dance is at the bowling alley. Next weekend's dance might be a family picnic and softball game. Be strong, no choices! Everyone has too many choices, and the time has come for you to select the music.

Become the dance instructor in your children's dances with life. Show them the joy of the rumba; learn the tango with your spouse, and give your kids something to giggle about! Teach everyone to practice their steps and then bring everyone together as one and let the music play.

Exercises

1. Smile at a stranger during rush hour and watch the re-action.
2. When you are communicating, notice the facial ex-pressions and body language of the people in your most important relationships.
3. Go dancing and notice how others respond to you as you get closer to them.

For their inspiration and guidance with the material in this chapter, many thanks go to:

Gladys Eaton. For teaching me how to dance.

Saracen Restaurant. For providing a wonderful environment for adults who love to dance.

Decade. For providing an uplifting setting in NYC for me to meet some dynamic women.

Michele Moretti & The Edge. For providing great music at Gigi's in Mizner Park and making me feel welcome in Boca Raton in the fall of 2004.

Abbe Aroshas. For being my first dance partner in Florida and showing me that dancing takes us into a different world.

Wealthy Profile #6

Retired entrepreneur, 62, married with a thirty-year-old daughter, a twenty-eight-year-old son, and a two-year-old granddaughter. Lives in Palm Beach, FL. He is very active in the Republican Party and devotes the majority of his time supporting candidates and raising money to forward the cause. He values his family so much that he missed an opportunity to have a private reception with the President of the United States because he didn't want to miss his granddaughter's birthday. He enjoys tennis, fine dining, and reading. He sold his business for over $25 million at age forty-six. He is persistent, but in a very light-hearted way. He is active in three charitable organizations and has donated well over one million dollars over the last few years. When he was in business, he gave opportunities to several young people to be in senior management positions, based on their willingness to work and learn how to be more effective. He has been married for over thirty-five years.

CHAPTER 9

Philanthropy as a Passion

Once the heart stops and attempts at resuscitation fail, it's all over—we're gone. I maintain that there are a lot of people living among us who are still breathing and have a pulse, but who are already long gone.

Remember the "Stop, Look, and Smile" exercise I told you to try? I wish something could be done to revive every commuter hurrying past my office building during rush hour in the sea of zombies. I want to remind them that smiles are needed. We have a lot of unfinished business to tend to: ending world hunger, finding cures to diseases that take our loved ones away too soon, educating our youth . . .

How much time do you presently devote to philanthropic endeavors?

Is there more you could do to help others?

For me, philanthropy is at the heart of a purpose-driven life and *The Passion for Success*. I am called to action when something moves me on a deep level. Because I lost my mother to cancer, I support organizations with a mission to find a cure. I have also volunteered my time at a summer camp for children who suffer from the disease, and, in honor of my mother's birthday, I hosted a party to celebrate her life and raise money for the American Cancer Society.

What cause would motivate you to give more of your time and money?

I know wealthy individuals who have a passion for opera, and they are patrons of the arts. They want to preserve and promote the cultural arts so they can continue to enjoy the performances of world-class singers, musicians, and conductors. They want to instill their love of opera in the hearts of their children and grandchildren.

Philanthropy is about recognizing a need somewhere in the world and providing a solution to it. You might contribute resources such as money to fund an initiative, an office where volunteers can hold their meetings, *pro bono* counsel, or your personal network of people who can give their time along with you.

True philanthropy is giving without expecting anything in return. It's about more than getting your name engraved on a wall—in fact the purest philanthropy is carried out with little or no fanfare. Those who give anonymously do so because their reward is not recognition, it's the satisfaction of knowing that their gift made a difference.

Do yourself a favor and don't dismiss what I am relating to you about cultivating philanthropic habits into your own life. Even if you think you don't have time to volunteer or money to give, you do.

The citizens of the world learned an invaluable lesson about humanity in the months following the events of September 11, 2001, the tsunami that struck Indonesia in 2004, and Hurricane Katrina that devastated New Orleans in 2005. We witnessed unprecedented giving.

People reevaluated their lives after those disasters. These are real examples of epiphanies. No matter how busy we may have been up until those moments, we stopped and took action. We were nicer to our families, friends, and coworkers. We sent money to the American Red Cross and other charities. Men and women from all over the world came to the disaster sites and did whatever they could to help the rescue effort. Some stayed for many months.

We all have a natural inclination to want to help another person who is in trouble. We want something positive to come out of a tragedy so we can attribute a greater meaning to it. This is one way we channel our positive energy and strive to make a difference.

One of my clients was an investment banker who had been making a couple million dollars a year. Although he had achieved financial success, he wanted more out of life. Working and traveling all the time, he didn't have a wife or children. After 9/11, he left his job and moved to Washington DC to work for a non-profit organization because he wanted his life to have more meaning.

Did you hear the wake-up calls on 9/11 and after the tsunami and hurricanes? If you heard your alarm go off, did you get up and take action, or did you press the snooze button?

If you sincerely want to experience an extraordinary life, don't use the snooze!

When you finally do get involved, don't just give to get. While your money will help the beneficiaries of the charity that receives your donation, you'll still feel empty. Lots of rich people are motivated to give because they have an ulterior motive. I know many businesspeople who will buy a table at a charitable event because they want to meet prospective clients and get a deal out of attending the function. They get dressed up, go to the great party, and have a few drinks. This is socially conscious networking; it's not philanthropy. Of course, it's OK to network at charitable events as I've just described, but be true to yourself about why you are there. And understand that it doesn't count as part of your philanthropic work according to *The Passion for Success.*

Many people practice checkbook philanthropy. They receive a fund-raising solicitation in the mail and they write a check for a nominal donation to the charity—with an explicit request for a receipt! Don't let me dissuade you from writing that check, just give a little more of yourself the next time.

Take time to learn more about the organization, its mission, and more ways you can help. Connect to your giving with your heart and your mind. Try it. You won't believe the difference you'll feel when you become emotionally involved with a cause and the people you help. This is how giving becomes fulfilling and develops into purpose-driven philanthropy.

One of the best ways to experience a deep sense of fulfillment from your personal philanthropy is to participate in programs with the direct beneficiaries of the particular charitable organizations you support. Be sure you get involved with an issue, cause, and people you really care about because if you spend your time, energy, and money on something you aren't passionate about, you will quickly lose interest.

Causes that fight cancer, help children, and promote education are where I devote most of my energy because I am passionate about each one. If you are an animal lover, an organization dedicated to protecting the welfare of animals may be an excellent avenue for you to explore as you become more charitably inclined. After researching the organization, you may decide you want to volunteer to take care of a pet that was abandoned until a permanent home can be found, or you might use your talents as a writer to produce a newsletter for the non-profit.

If you have considerable means, you might set-up a foundation and earmark monies for various programs that benefit the causes you champion.

There are endless possibilities and pathways to finding your philanthropic passion. To help you discern what pursuits would turn you on, ask yourself the following three questions:

1. In what areas do I want to make an impact on the world to make it a better place?
2. What inspires me and moves me, even to the point of tears, when I hear about it?
3. What tragedies (illnesses, events) have touched my family and friends?

Your answers to these questions may provide you with a good starting point. Also, once your mind is considering a cause for you to support, you'll be surprised how many opportunities will come your way.

Throughout *The Passion for Success* I have tried to impress upon you that taking action in life without feeling passionate, moved, and excited is really a waste of time. When you do things out of a sense of obligation, these activities eventually feel burdensome and irritating. You quickly begin to wonder why you are spending your efforts on something you don't particularly care about, and you can't wait to go home. That kind of charity doesn't feel good for anybody.

As I mentioned earlier, helping children is something I care deeply about. I was asked to sit on the Board of the Friends of Island Academy. FOIA provides job training, anger management, counseling, education, a GED program, mentoring, and youth leadership development to at-risk adolescents before they are released from Rikers Island. FOIA is impacting these kids because recidivism has been dramatically reduced with this program.

About five or six years ago, I was sitting at a sushi bar and started talking with the couple sitting next to me. We got on the subject of tennis and what we do professionally. The couple's son also played competitive tennis, and the gentleman owned a menswear company, which produced a label I had been wearing since I first entered the business world.

As we kept talking, the wife told me about the non-profit she created and invited me to become involved. She liked me and thought that as a person of color I might be a good role model for the kids their organization helps. They were in the process of restructuring their Board, and I was in the right place at the right time.

While I wasn't thinking specifically about helping teenagers in the prison system, I cared about kids and I wanted to get involved. Joining the Board of a charitable organization is quite an honor, but it typically demands a great deal of a participant's time. So if it had been geared toward a cause that was outside my primary areas of philanthropic interest, I most likely would have declined his offer. My involvement with FOIA, despite the time it takes, has been extremely rewarding. I am so grateful to have met that lovely couple who became my friends, and I still play tennis with their son.

Through tennis I became familiar with another organization that helps children with cancer, Camp Adventure. The Cartier Grand Slam Tennis Challenge in the Hamptons, organized by the American Cancer Society, benefits the camp. Some of the rounds and events are actually held on the estates of residents in the Hamptons who open their homes for the charity.

Camp Adventure is an incredible place on Shelter Island, located off Long Island's east end. Children visit the camp for a week together with their healthy brothers and sisters. The

American Cancer Society pays all expenses. When you go to the camp, you can't help but be moved by all of the children playing, laughing, and having fun together.

Adult volunteers, many who are busy with their careers, take a week off and give up their precious vacation time to work at the camp and care for the kids. Many of the adults' lives have been affected by cancer, and these incredible people want to do something to make the children's lives better. Their reward is making a smile appear on the face of a child who may not have smiled in years because of illness.

At Camp Adventure I saw the kids enjoying face painting, soccer, softball, basketball, and a circus! I couldn't help being profoundly changed by what I saw. Every year the kids have a ceremony and pay tribute to the children who were at the camp in previous years, but are no longer with us. I met a healthy boy who told me he was feeling sad that his own brother may not be back at camp next year.

Camp Adventure changed my life. This experience touched me in such a way that I want more people to get involved in the fight against cancer, and in loving and comforting the children afflicted with this disease. It simply isn't enough to open our checkbooks and send our money to take care of the problems of this world. We need to connect to the people who need our help with both our hearts and minds.

Once you discover how it feels to give your time and money to causes you are passionate about, you will want to keep doing it. You will also become enriched by your associations with others who share your passion for a particular cause. It is amazing how you form an instant bond with other like-minded charitable people when you're in the philanthropic mode.

However you choose to take action, whether you serve on a committee, build homes for the homeless, or organize an annual dinner for the local hospice, you will have the opportunity to meet many good people. As you work alongside others who share your mission or vision for making the world a better place, you will get to know them in an intimate way.

Many philanthropic men and women are solution oriented, driven, and passionate. They are also kind-hearted, generous, and energetic. These individuals are the kind of people you would be fortunate to have in your inner Circle of Success.

Look for opportunities to make a difference in the world and take action that is consistent with your basic values. If you follow this advice, you will discover something powerful that will move you and change your life.

We get messages and reminders that we are needed all the time. Last summer I met a homeless woman on Fire Island who was selling necklaces and bracelets she made out of seashells. She asked me to buy one, and I did. That necklace now hangs on the rearview mirror of my car where I can see it every day. When I focus on that necklace, I can remember the look in that woman's eyes, and I am grateful for all that I have been given.

I hope you will remember this powerful quote from the *Sefer Hasidim:* "The Almighty has willed that there will be two hands in the matter of charity, one that gives and one that receives. Be thankful that yours is the one that gives."

Keep watching and listening for the messages life sends you. Don't delay your giving until you retire, your kids are out of the house, you have more money, or you have more time. Start doing good for others now.

Teach your children to be charitable. Bring them with you when you volunteer at a soup kitchen or donate gifts to the U.S. Marines' Toys for Tots campaign during the holidays. Teaching your kids that they can make a difference in the lives of others is one of the greatest gifts you will ever give them.

Exercises

1. Answer the questions on page 104.
2. Volunteer for at least an hour per week in a different charity for four consecutive weeks.
3. Donate ten percent of your gross income to the charities/people of your choice for three months, and note the emotional and financial impact in your own life.

For their inspiration and guidance with the material in this chapter, many thanks go to:

Cindy Sulzberger. For devoting your life to your children and philanthropic causes.

Sidney Witter-Daire. For genuinely caring about the welfare of others.

Marc Saffren. For teaching affluent individuals to utilize their resources to make the world a better place.

Christopher Williams. For being a successful investment banker who gives back.

Julie Ratner. For identifying problems in the world and rallying others around the solution.

CHAPTER 10

Overcoming Fear

When President Franklin D. Roosevelt addressed our nation in his first inaugural address, he asserted the now famous words, "The only thing we have to fear is fear itself."

I'm sure you have heard this truism many times. But have you ever stopped and really thought about the meaning of this familiar statement?

I urge you to take a moment to reread (and really think about) FDR's words:

The *ONLY* thing we have to fear *IS* <u>FEAR</u> itself.

President Roosevelt's message is as true today as it was in 1933—in the depth of one of the most trying times in our history, the Great Depression. Yet, while our parents and grandparents triumphed over poverty and record levels of unemployment, fear remains one of the most powerful forces on our planet.

How does fear hold us in its tight grip? In this chapter, we take a hard look at the impact fear has on our lives. It is essential to recognize fear in its various forms in order to overcome it. Once you have a greater awareness of the insidious ways fear works, you can meet it head-on and disarm it; you can free yourself to pursue your life's passions with confidence.

Fear is an equal opportunity emotion. It strikes at the hearts of men and women of all ages, colors, religions, education levels, and economic levels. This debilitating survival mechanism is hardwired into our psyche because it served to protect our ancestors (the ones who lived in caves and hunted for their food). Neither evolution nor money can eradicate fear. Every one of the 513 successful people who participated in the interviews for *The Passion for Success* attested to having fears—big and small. But what separates these individuals from everyone else is their "no excuses" attitude. These life champions don't allow their fears to stop them. They take deliberate action in the face of their fears until they prevail.

How you choose to deal with your fears will determine the level of success you will achieve in life. You do have a choice. You can allow fear to completely stifle you and shut you down, or you can channel your fear into a motivating force that will propel you to take action.

Have you seen the 1998 film, *As Good as It Gets*? In this Academy Award-winning movie, Jack Nicholson portrays a character who suffers from Obsessive-Compulsive Disorder (OCD). Melvin is afraid of germs and stepping on cracks in the sidewalk. His phobias prevent him from enjoying life and getting close to people, until he meets a woman (played by Helen Hunt) and they fall in love. As difficult as it is to overcome his fears and his illness, Melvin is determined to succeed and get his girl.

How do you want to respond to the fears that hold you back?

What would motivate you to find a way to overcome your fears?

If you are in sales (or any profession that requires you to bring in business), you may be afraid of rejection, but if you don't ask your prospects for their business, your outcome is certain failure. If you don't get out from behind your desk, you'll eventually have bigger worries—such as losing your job (or business) and your home. I don't know about you, but I'd rather learn how to overcome the fear of rejection!

If you are genuinely afraid of not being able to keep your house, you'll wake up in the morning and take the actions necessary to succeed at your job and make money, even if that means finding another job that you like better.

If you are afraid of rejection but your fear of being alone for the rest of your life is even greater, I am confident you will eventually overcome your fear of asking people out.

No one likes rejection. But it's a common occurrence in life, and you need to remember it's not personal. You may have the

greatest solution for a client, but they chos(
product or service in order to save money. Yo\
Right," but you've got your eyes on someone w\
on someone else. You are the ideal candidate f
you're considered overqualified.

Just as you'll need to overcome your fear and put yourself
out there to make a sale, to find and marry your soul mate, or to
land your dream job, you also need to learn how to bounce back
from failure. Champions succeed more than everyone else because they respond to every win and loss by getting back in the
game. They don't like to watch life from the sidelines, and they
know it's not productive to cry over spilled milk.

A major inhibitor for many people is their fear of looking
bad, inferior, or foolish, because they have so much vested in always trying to look good. Nobody in the world wants to look
bad. But, when your level of fear and self-consciousness inter-
feres with your work and your relationships, it's time to address
the issue. This fear of making a fool of oneself is why so many
adults are afraid of public speaking.

The best way to overcome your fear of public speaking is by
doing it, as is true of everything else. The more you do something, the more comfortable and confident you become. Many
people join organizations such as Toastmasters International,
where they can practice with others who also want to develop
their public speaking skills.

In my sales workshops, I often teach people an exercise I
found to be very helpful when I was young. Whether you are
walking alone on the street or entering a boardroom full of people, look each person in their eyes and silently repeat to yourself,
"I am afraid of you, and I know you are afraid of me." This is an
excellent reminder that we are all human, and we all have fears.

Let's face it, fear is a given! So you need to ask yourself, "Is
fear going to stop me or is it going to propel me?" Many great
ancestors, present-day leaders, and entrepreneurs view their
fears as tests that measure their will to succeed. These individuals see "challenges" they must overcome rather than "obstacles" that will defeat them. Success is about attitude.

Successful entrepreneurs and salespeople face the same

potential for rejection and failure as everyone else. In fact, they have probably heard more "nos" in order to get the number of "yeses" needed to achieve their goals. Success in sales (as in life) is very much a numbers game.

One of my colleagues in the insurance industry says he celebrates every time he gets a "no" from a prospect. In fact, he has actually calculated how much a no is worth to him because he understands every no gets him one step closer to his next yes. He has totally disarmed and depersonalized rejection. And he has made his job into a game—what a great way to transform one's mindset! He remains in control because he made up the rules of his own game.

The object of his game is clear: to get the number of yeses he needs to "win" the sales and earn all of his "prize" money. His game strategy is to see enough people in order to create enough opportunities to ask qualified prospects to buy insurance. And, just like every great champion, he stays focused after every lost point in order to ultimately win the big "match" points.

If your livelihood depends on your ability to close deals, you've got to get out there and put yourself into the game. If you are reluctant to make the phone calls needed to get appointments with your business prospects, you'll have no chance of succeeding. If that's the case, you either need to find another line of work or you need a major attitude adjustment to begin thinking like a winner.

Your competitors are hungry and talented. If their desire to win the customers' business is greater than your own, they will win and you will lose. That's the reality you should fear!

Let's assume you aren't afraid to get into the game and that you're actually somewhat of a superstar presenter. I won't be sold on your selling skills until I hear you ask for the sale. That may seem harsh, but there are many business owners and sales professionals who tell me they put together brilliant presentations about their superior product or service offerings, yet they aren't closing business deals. It's probably because they are afraid to ask for the business.

It's amazing how many sales people will spend their days and late nights creating a fabulous PowerPoint presentation, rehearse it with their team at work or significant other at home, prepare beautiful coordinating collateral material, and then spend hours in their big meeting without ever asking for the sale.

The punch line is that the sales professional who follows your highly educational and informative presentation will typically get the sale because he or she went one simple step further and asked the client to sign the deal. You set it up, and someone else closes the deal—it happens all the time.

Why do you think law firms have rainmakers? Why do you think those individuals make so much money? It's simple: Without someone sticking his or her neck out and asking for the work, it doesn't matter how accomplished the partners are—no clients, no money, no firm.

More and more, accountants seek to expand into financial services. Many fail miserably at their attempts because they are too uncomfortable and lack the training to ask clients to buy.

So why do you suppose salespeople and entrepreneurs make so much money? Are they any smarter than doctors, lawyers, or college professors? Of course not—it's really about risk and reward. Typically, our returns are tied to the level of risk we are willing to take.

Successful salespeople and entrepreneurs weren't born with thicker skin; they learned how to toughen up. Innately, nobody likes to hear someone say no. But, if you would prefer to schmooze with clients over lunch rather than sit in a cubicle and number crunch, you must be prepared to hear that two-letter word many times.

I've learned not to take rejection personally because the insurance business (like everything else) is a numbers game. So many factors enter into a successful sale: the timing, my delivery, the other person's mood, how the prospect feels about money, etc.

Whenever I hear the word no, after I've tried to overcome any legitimate objections, I really like to use another word that starts with N: "next." I developed this attitude from what I learned playing tennis. It's just not worth it to get angry at a call. If someone makes a bad call and gives the point to my opponent, it's more productive for me to spend my time focused on the next game than to argue about why I should have won the last one.

/ When I win an account and someone tells me I've done a great job, I never hesitate to ask that person to tell family and friends about me. Successful sales professionals always ask for referrals. They know their happy clients will gladly spread the word to others in need of the same services, just as we tell others about the new restaurant or great movie we saw the other night.

Do you ask for referrals in your business? If not, why don't you? What's the worst thing that could happen if you asked your client to send you some business? Is it that they might say, "no"? It is time you learned how to accept *no* and move on.

You'll have an easier time letting go of *no* by reminding yourself that it's not all about you. Besides, if your "happy" clients tell you *no* when you ask them to refer you, you need to deal with something more important than your ego. This "no" is a warning sign that your relationship is in trouble. If you value the individual's business, it is incumbent upon you to ask what's wrong so you can take care of the issue and save the account.

How you act to resolve your customer's issue will determine the fate of your relationship. You cannot be defensive. You must be open to criticism and allow yourself to hear your client's feedback. Even if you can't repair the specific situation, you need to prevent it from happening again.

Keep in mind that while many circumstances may be out of your control, you always control how you choose to respond to your client's message. Thank your clients for bringing their concerns to your attention and giving you the opportunity to make everything right.

Sometimes the most difficult cases bring the greatest rewards. And, when you keep your clients informed of how you are working on their behalf to solve the problem, you are strengthening your relationship.

At the risk of sounding trite, no matter what happens, honesty is always the best policy. You may be petrified to tell your clients that their issue is still unresolved or mortified if it can't be fixed, but it is essential that you communicate openly and truthfully. Your relationship and your reputation depend upon your word.

Ironically, while many customers fail to tell others about their positive experiences with a salesperson or company, they tell everyone about all the problems they encounter—in great detail, right down to naming the individual who either did nothing or was rude.

Successful people become successful by doing the right things. They attract clients, friends, business partners, and life partners because they have a high degree of self-confidence (not arrogance).

Self-confidence is attractive! Would you be attracted to someone who is afraid or appears insecure? Would you hire someone who appears nervous throughout the job interview? Would you buy something from anyone who isn't confident about himself or the product?

Do you have confidence in your knowledge, skills, and abilities? Are you someone who is a good friend, employee/employer, and a "good catch"?

If you answered no to either of these questions, then you must first do the work to develop yourself in the areas that need improvement. Once you can look yourself in the mirror and sincerely say yes to both of these questions, others will say yes to you, too.

A great exercise to build your self-esteem is something you can do each morning when you first wake up. Get up, and walk over to your mirror. Smile at yourself and say, "You're GREAT!" If you do this every morning for thirty days straight, you'll be amazed at how much better you will feel about yourself.

When you improve your self-esteem, everything will begin to fall into place. Self-esteem is closely related to faith—faith in yourself as well as faith in a greater power. When you truly have faith, you are able to trust that you will be alright no matter what happens and that everything will work out for the best. This faith will give you the confidence to get in an elevator, fly on a plane, jump off the high diving board, go on the interview, get married, bring children into this world, and so much more.

If your fear is justifiable (you are unprepared for the test, you've never made a presentation before, or you once got stuck in an elevator), you'll need to address the problem so you can ensure your success in the future. Study before the next test, practice making presentations, ask your best friend to ride in an elevator with you until you become more comfortable.

If it is important to you to overcome your fear, you can find a way to do so. Each time you overcome a fear, you will feel empowered. Empowerment and self-confidence go hand in hand.

It's vital that you focus on your goals rather than your fears. When you concentrate all of your energy on achieving your objectives, your mind will automatically set a course toward that end and kick into problem-solving mode. But, if you are fixated on obstacles and obsessing about failure, you will inadvertently set your mind's autopilot onto the wrong course.

Remember, if you are driving your car and you suddenly see you are heading toward a tree, you must immediately set your sight on a safe spot and steer in that direction. If you keep staring at the tree, you'll hit the tree. If you want to make a good impression on a date, you must visualize yourself doing everything right.

Tony Robbins, a master of motivation, is a proponent of the power of visualization. His books, seminars, and videos teach techniques for "Peak Performance" and "Unleashing the Power Within" (which is the power of our thoughts).

Ask his seminar participants to tell you what it was like to walk across burning coals. This incredible exercise is a metaphor Robbins uses to demonstrate the power of our minds over virtually anything. It is a life-changing experience for everyone who walks barefoot across the red-hot coals because once you've done it and see there isn't even one blister on your feet, you begin to realize how you can overcome your fear and do anything you set your mind to do.

How much are you limiting yourself—and your success—by the things you tell yourself? What if you changed what you tell yourself? What would happen if you believed in yourself? How much better would your life be if you conquered your fears?

Don't let your fears stop you from experiencing life to

its fullest. Do you want anything to have that kind of power over you?

I challenge you to take on the fears that have stopped you from living the life you only dared to dream about until now.

Many wealthy individuals have faith that opportunities and things are put in their lives to help them serve a higher purpose. They don't struggle with fear of scarcity because they have a deep sense of abundance. They have confidence in their abilities to accomplish their good deeds, which may be acquiring the resources to start a business that will create jobs and a product or service that makes lives better.

Successful entrepreneurs aren't afraid of losing money because they know they have the knowledge and skills to make more money. Secure individuals who have a healthy self-esteem and faith aren't afraid of losing their possessions because they define a wealthy life as so much more than the accumulation of material things.

In contrast, many insecure rich people live in constant fear of losing everything they have—they're paranoid about getting robbed, sued, and so on. They worry about everything. Listen to their conversations. It's all very self-limiting; it's all about them and their sense of entitlement. They think the world owes them rather than seeing it the other way around.

The wealthy think about the world outside of themselves. They genuinely want to make a difference in the world, and their wealth is often a by-product of their efforts to do good things. They are excited, extroverted, and filled with good energy. When you possess good energy and your intentions are in the right place, you will find the support needed to achieve your objectives. Fear is not an option for life's champions because they have too much they want to do and can't afford to spend their time and energy on such foolishness.

When you view the responsibilities for getting what you want out of life as residing anywhere outside of yourself, you will have absolutely no control over your life. And when you feel you have no control over your life, you will be fearful.

This is often the case when people work for someone else. Most employees constantly worry about getting laid off or fired, and they abdicate the responsibility for how much money they are going to make by letting their employers determine their worth. They legitimately fear they aren't going to get a raise or the bonus they deserve because they gave up control.

I'm not saying you shouldn't ever be an employee. I am saying you need to wake up and have confidence in yourself and the value you bring to a company and your clients. If you truly add value, you should be fairly compensated. If you have a healthy self-esteem and know that another firm will pay you the fair market value for your contributions, then you will be coming from a position of strength and abundance. When you have arrived at that level of awareness, you will be ready to leave and ask others if they have an opening for someone of your caliber to join their team.

When we buy into the limiting fears that have entrapped us for twenty, thirty, or forty-plus years, there is nothing that can set us free except our own minds. The truth that sets you free lies within your beautiful, inner self. It's there waiting for you to call upon its power so you will have the ability to take action, realize your dreams, and make your contribution to this world. When you arrive at this ultimate truth, you will be rewarded with success in all aspects of your life. You will enjoy the fruits of your prosperity with your family and friends, and you will have more than you can imagine for giving to the philanthropic causes that need your help.

Exercises

1. Do the "You are great" exercise on page 115 for thirty consecutive days.
2. Ask the most successful person you know to share his or her secrets for overcoming fear.
3. Make a list of all your fears and ask a member of your inner circle to create an exercise that requires you to face each of your fears head on.

For their inspiration and guidance with the material in this chapter, many thanks go to:

Ava Roosevelt. For your courage in exploring what can make you stronger.

Barbara Buxton. For becoming a lawyer after a life as a doctor's wife.

Kevin Ellis. For moving to Kansas to start a new life with your wife.

William Katz. For consistently challenging yourself to be more effective in sales.

Karl Wexler. For handling physical challenges and sharing your story to inspire others.

Wealthy Profile #7

Real estate developer, 43, married with a nine-year-old daughter and a seven-year-old son. Lives in New York City. His father is a member of the Forbes 400, yet he has developed a successful business on his own. He is on the board of several charities, which have a direct impact on the Jewish and Upper Westside communities. He donates over $400,000 a year to various causes. He loves golf, music, and spending time with his family. He exercises five times a week. He has led a privileged life; however, he truly understands the old adage "to whom much is given, much is expected." He is committed to improving race relations. He spends one month in the Hamptons each summer to bond with his family and de-stress.

CHAPTER 11

Exercises to Build the Self-Confidence Muscle

What is the difference between the meanings of *self-esteem* and *self-confidence*?

Self-esteem is "a feeling of pride in oneself and being worthy of esteem and respect."[1]

Self-confidence is "freedom from doubt; belief in yourself and your abilities."[2]

How much pride do you have in yourself? A lot, some, none?

Are you worthy of respect (from yourself and others)?

Do you typically doubt yourself and your abilities?

In the last chapter, we looked at fear and the various ways fears prevent us from fully experiencing life. I hope you will always remember this message: it's your choice to either allow your fears to permanently paralyze you, or do what is necessary to overcome them.

The objective of this chapter is to assess your level of self-esteem and gain a greater awareness of the impact self-esteem has on the quality of every aspect of your life.

Before reading on, look again at the questions at the beginning of the chapter and consider your answers to each of those questions. If you have pride, self-respect, and self-confidence, good for you! You will have what it takes to pursue your passions and succeed in your endeavors.

If you realize you do not have a great deal of pride, respect for yourself, or confidence in your abilities, you will need to work harder to build your self-esteem muscle. How can you ask others to respect you and believe in your abilities, unless you do? I once heard a seminar speaker tell his audience, "You cannot sell what you do not own!" How true.

Much of our self-esteem is formed during our early years when we don't have the coping skills and adult perspective to deal with pain. Maybe you were told you were stupid or you'd never amount to anything. If you were the new kid on the block, other kids may have teased you; maybe you weighed too much or wore glasses . . .

But you have to get a grip! Successful people know that it's not about what happened to us as kids or adolescents that determine our destiny; it's how we respond to each adversity that ultimately influences our success and happiness. I encourage you to figure out what you need to do to resolve your feelings, so you can answer each of those questions at the beginning of this chapter in the affirmative.

One final note before we begin the first exercise: I view all exercise as essential activity for our well-being. Because exercise is so critical to the quality of life, I think of ways to make it fun rather than regarding it as a chore.

I deliberately avoided the term "workout" when titling this chapter because you may have an aversion to the word. The exercises presented in this chapter are a series of games and number games we were taught in school when we were learning spelling, vocabulary, and math.

No moaning and groaning allowed! And no cheating!

Exercise 1—Love Poem

* Required equipment: pen, pad of lined paper, stopwatch.

1. Title your first page, "Why I Love Myself—Let Me Count the Ways."
2. Set your stopwatch alarm for ten minutes.
3. Press start.
4. Make a list of all of the things that you love about yourself (it doesn't have to rhyme). Use as much detail and explanation as you can. Let it flow. Use as much paper as you need.

Exercise 2—Put it on the table

* Required equipment: pen, pad of lined paper, stopwatch.

1. Title this page, "What I Hate About Myself."
2. Reset your stopwatch alarm for ten minutes.
3. Press start.
4. Write down every reason you have not to like yourself (whether it's because you're cheap, a cheater, or a liar—nothing is out of bounds). Pretend you're gossiping about someone who drives you crazy, but that someone just happens to be you! Remember, you can hate the sin and love the sinner.
5. Don't hold back. Be truthful.

Exercise 3—S.W.O.T.

* Required equipment: six separate pieces of paper.

1. At the top of the first page, write: "My Strengths."
2. At the top of the second page, write: "My Weaknesses."
3. At the top of the third page, write "My Opportunities."
4. At the top of the fourth page, write "My Threats."
5. Under "My Strengths," list every positive personality attribute that serves you well (e.g., I am a good listener; I am a good provider).
6. Under "My Weaknesses," list facets of your personality that you know have room for improvement (e.g., I have a short temper).
7. Under "My Opportunities," list realistic reasons you have to be optimistic about your future (e.g., I have a new job offer; my friends want me to join them on a cruise in Alaska; I just met a terrific person; I'm going to be a parent or grandparent).
8. Under "My Threats," list any potential obstacles to achieving happiness and a passionate, successful life (e.g., My parents or spouse keep telling me to stop dreaming; I'm in debt).

9. Review your answers for "My Weaknesses." On a new sheet of paper, list every action you can take to overcome each weakness.

10. Review your answers for "My Threats." On a new sheet of paper, list every action you can take to overcome each obstacle.

Time Out for a Reminder: In order to gain the maximum benefit from each self-esteem exercise, it's up to you to give each one your all. If I were working as your personal trainer, I'd coach you to push yourself to the max for each exercise. Don't write down a "3 lb. dumbbell" answer, when you are capable of heavier lifting—go for the burn! No pain, no gain!

Exercise 4—Make a good deed deposit

* Required equipment: pen, scrap paper, small box.

Do this every day.

1. Before going to sleep each night, write down a good deed that you've done—something positive you've put into the world, no matter how small it may seem.

2. Fold the sheet of paper, and put it into your box.

I love this exercise because it helps us to focus on doing good things and keeping a record. I chose for my box a *matzo* box of *mitzvot* (the Hebrew word for "good deeds"), which is one of my most precious possessions. I find that making a daily deposit into my good deed bank also helps me to hold myself more accountable for my actions and some of the choices I make.

Read a good deed note whenever you need a reminder that you're a good soul who makes good things happen. (There's nothing like having a reserve of good deeds that you can draw upon when you're in a time of need.) Whenever I read about one of the good things I've done in the past to help someone less fortunate or to leave this world a better place, I'm able to recall all of the details of that incident—the person I helped, our conversation, the smiles, and how good we both felt.

Exercise 5—Muhammad Ali's "I'm the Greatest"

* Required equipment: a mirror.

Muhammad Ali is one of the all-time greatest heavyweight boxing champions. Many people consider this larger-than-life man to be *the* greatest. In fact, Ali himself was notorious for proclaiming to opponents, interviewers, and fans alike, "I'm the greatest."

Back in the 1960s and 1970s, Ali's public self-aggrandizing put some people off. That didn't matter to Muhammad Ali because he was saying it for his own ears and mind to hear. His famous mantra pumped him up and mentally prepared him to take on his opponent.

I'm not suggesting that you go out and tell everyone you meet that you're the greatest. This exercise is meant just for you. It's an internal process. I want you to get to the point where you can look yourself in the eye when you're in front of a mirror and tell yourself, "You're great"—and really mean it.

This is about acknowledging your own greatness. If you were to go out and tell others that you're great, they'd consider you arrogant. Truly great people (with the exception of Ali) do not brag. Great people are recognizable because they radiate self-confidence (not arrogance). Aren't qualities such as intelligence, generosity, and kindness apparent right away?

I'm not suggesting you are greater than anyone else. When you come to the realization that you have inner greatness, you will also begin to recognize the inner greatness in others.

Now, go over to your mirror, look yourself directly in the eyes, and repeat to yourself, "You're great!"

Do this empowering exercise faithfully each and every morning. You'll notice a difference in your confidence within thirty days as your self-image accepts this new message and permanently records it over the old one.

After you have completed Exercise 5 for thirty consecutive days, you are ready for the intermediate and advanced exercises.

Exercises 6 and 7—Advanced "Ali" training

* Required equipment: a mirror.

1. For the next thirty days, go to your mirror and say, "I love you."

After successfully completing your intermediate mirror exercise, you can move on to the advanced mirror exercise for another thirty days.

2. Go to your mirror and say, "I love you because _____." Fill in the blank with reasons you love yourself.

If you believe you are deserving of love and you genuinely want to have loving relationships with your spouse, children, siblings, grandchildren, and close friends, you must first be able to love yourself.

Love in all its forms is an essential element in a passionate, successful, wealthy life. You may be surprised by the transformation that will take place when you succeed at building your self-confidence muscle and finally love yourself unconditionally. Your inner self-confidence will radiate outward, and you will attract the kinds of people you want to have in your life. And the quality of your relationships with family and friends will improve beyond measure.

There is an infinite supply of love in the universe—you just need to tap into it. When you do, you'll be able to give and receive love in ways you never dreamed.

Exercise 8 — The Ed Koch

* Required equipment: pen, pad of paper, tape recorder, your Circle of Success.

Former New York City Mayor Ed Koch inspired this exercise. Koch wanted to be the best mayor he could be, so he always asked people, "How am I doing?" Koch was an effective leader because he had passion, vision, healthy self-esteem, and the sincere desire to succeed. He was passionate about his job and New York City.

For this exercise, sit down with four or five of the people who are closest to you (and whose opinions you respect).

1. Explain to each person individually that you are making positive changes in your life, and you would appreciate honest, constructive feedback.
2. Ask each person the following questions. Record their answers.
   a. What are my strengths?
   b. What are my weaknesses?
   c. When have I disappointed you and how?
   d. What would you do or say differently if I weren't in the room?
   e. Is there anything else you'd like to add?
3. Study each answer carefully. Allow yourself to receive each message and determine what you can do to better.
4. Handwrite a thank-you note, and send it to all the people who helped you with this exercise. Let them know how much you value their love, friendship and opinions.

When you can possess a healthy self-esteem, you will bring a complete person into your personal and professional relationships. This will enable you to sustain successful relationships with quality individuals. (But you will only function at this higher level when you do the work necessary to know you are deserving of this kind of love and success).

Once you get to this stage in your personal development, the possibilities are limitless.

For their inspiration and guidance with the material in this chapter, many thanks go to:

Daniel Eaton. For sharing your beliefs and reading the works of masters to reinforce them.

Doug Levine. For inspiring others by founding Crunch Fitness and making exercise fun.

Dexter Wadsworth. For walking with confidence even in challenging times.

Felicia Goldberg. For believing in yourself even when fear was present in your family and friends.

Amy Kaplan. For being beautiful inside and out.

CHAPTER 12

Taking Risk

Imagine a life without risk . . . a world in which we are 100 percent safe, twenty-four hours a day, seven days a week . . . Wouldn't that be wonderful?

Even though a recent news report cited a statistic that estimates the probability of dying in a car crash is 1 in 100, I'm not about to give up that mode of transportation.

I'd rather invest in a diversified portfolio of stocks, mutual funds, insurance, real estate, and other places where my money can grow, than stash my money under the mattress.

I will always seek opportunities to play with better tennis players, even though I might lose a match, because I want to improve my game and enjoy being challenged.

And if you think I'd ever hesitate to ask a woman to dance for fear she may say no, you haven't read the last twelve chapters of this book! Did you even read the full title? *The Passion for Success—The Mindset of Champions.* This book is about living life to its fullest and approaching everything life has to offer as a champion. And life's champions take risks. In the words of one of sports' greatest champions, Michael Jordan, "I can accept failure, but I can't accept not trying."

I do not know any self-made wealthy individuals who became successful by playing it safe. Do you? Can you name any hero in the history of our world who managed to effect change without taking any risk? Individually and collectively, we cannot grow if we shy away from risk.

What would the status of South African Blacks be today if Nelson Mandela hadn't risked his life and given up his personal freedom to fight for justice and human rights? This great man spent twenty-seven years in prison before his dream of equality became a possibility.

Only a generation ago, here in the United States, Dr. Martin Luther King, Jr. lost his life in his efforts to realize his dream:

> I have a dream that one day this nation will rise up and live out the true meaning of its creed: 'We hold these truths to be self-evident: that all men are created equal.' I have a dream that one day on the red hills of Georgia the sons of former slaves and the sons of former slave owners will be able to sit down together at a table of brotherhood. I have a dream that one day even the state of Mississippi, a desert state, sweltering with the heat of injustice and oppression, will be transformed into an oasis of freedom and justice. I have a dream that my four children will one day live in a nation where they will not be judged by the color of their skin but by the content of their character. I have a dream today . . ."

Can you imagine the courage and conviction Dr. King needed to deliver those words on the steps of the Lincoln Memorial in 1963? It must have been the same desire and determination that our forefathers had when they fought the American War of Independence against England. Independent-minded risk takers built our country and its economy, which is the world's largest. America's captains of industry have historically led the world with innovation. Social and political change, economic growth, and leadership all require taking risk.

The only way to achieve utopia as a society is to have faith—in yourself, humanity and God. With faith, we have the power to take necessary risks. To be clear, I am not suggesting your goal must be to become the next great national leader. Let the leaders you admire be your role models. Then add as many ordinary people as you can to this list. Perhaps your parents or grandparents came to the United States at great personal risk in order to give you and your children the opportunity for a better life. Maybe you know a fireman who is willing to put his life on the line every day. Every night on the evening news we are reminded that there are thousands of American servicemen and women fighting the war on terror and defending freedom.

After contemplating risks of life-and-death magnitude, consider:

- Breaking your everyday routine and trying something new.
- Asking your employer or client for more money (if you deserve it).
- Going out on the limb for someone who needs your help.
- Starting your own business.
- Moving into that bigger house.
- Admitting you were wrong and apologizing to someone you've hurt.
- Offering your honest opinion, even if it's contrary to what's popular.

While we can increase our tolerance for risk (especially when we are highly motivated), taking risks requires a healthy self-esteem. That is why Chapter 11 includes several exercises to help you increase your self-esteem. You may need to spend more time strengthening your self-esteem and self-confidence muscles before you strive to increase your capacity for taking risks.

How would you assess your current tolerance for risk? Select the choices that best describe your attitude today. There are no right answers, so be truthful!

1. I prefer to invest my money in:
   a. An FDIC savings account
   b. Mutual funds
   c. Start-up ventures
2. I want to be:
   a. A lifetime employee with my current employer
   b. A partner in this firm or another business
   c. The owner of my own company
3. If I were at the craps table at the Bellagio Hotel in Las Vegas, I would:
   a. Watch the action
   b. Bet the minimum for the table
   c. Put it all on Lucky Seven

If you answered "A" to each of these questions, then you are definitely someone who is most comfortable playing it safe.

If you answered "B" for each question, you can handle an average or slightly above-average amount of risk.

And, if your answers all came up "C," you are a risk-taker!

If your answers were mixed, you may be more confident taking greater risks in some areas of your life than others.

Your answers to these questions are not a serious scientific psychological profile. Nor is this about moving you from an "A" to a "C" type of risk-taker. The real objective is to honor the wisdom of "know thy self" and to support you as you step outside of your comfort zone to pursue your life's passions and set higher life goals.

If one of your ultimate dreams is to see the Great Wall of China, but you are afraid to fly to the other side of the world, how would you set out to overcome your fear and realize this goal?

Would you be willing to invest some of your savings in a riskier investment for a higher rate of return? If so, how much of your money would you invest? How much more of a return would you demand? How much more risk would you tolerate? What do you consider "safe"? How much is "too much" risk?

Corporations utilize the expertise of professional finance and risk managers to assess risk probabilities and outcomes, weigh the benefits of various tradeoffs, and maintain the right balance of risk necessary to achieve their stated growth and revenue objectives.

So let's look at the question of risk from another angle. If you were "John Doe, Inc." or "Mary Smith Corp.," you would need to determine your stated growth and revenue objectives, too. How much money do you want to make this year? How much more do you need to earn on your money to grow the value of your savings/assets and reach your growth objective?

Can you achieve your goals without increasing your level of personal risk? (If so, is it possible you have set your goals too low?)

If you want to increase your annual income from $75,000 to $100,000, you need to consider what you could do to make that happen. For example, you could:

- Ask for a raise.
- Look for a new job.
- Start a business at home to generate additional income.
- Play the lottery.
- Tell your boss what your income goal is and discuss what you can do to earn the additional money.

Each of these choices requires different levels of risk. Also, the probability of achieving the additional $25,000 in income goal varies significantly as we compare the individual options. Common sense tells us that if you genuinely want the additional income, you must make choices based on the level of risk you are willing to take and on the likelihood that your actions will result in the desired outcome.

Winners do not take risks for the sake of taking risks. The mindset of a champion is having goals, creating a plan, and evaluating risk in the context of the reward.

There are also times when we take risks that are seemingly out of character. You may be the type of person who tries not to make waves at the office because you have a family counting on you to provide financially for its well-being. Yet, if you are asked to do something that goes against your character morally or ethically, you may decide it is worth risking your job to stand-up and say you object to doing it.

In this case, after weighing the risks associated with each option, you've determined it is safer to lose your current source of income (because you can always find another job). If you stay quiet so you can keep getting a paycheck from this company, you may be legally liable for your actions. Additionally, there is a high probability that you will jeopardize your health due to the stress of staying in this situation.

There are also circumstances in which we place ourselves at great risk because the consequences of not taking action are unthinkable. If your house was on fire and your children were inside, your instinct would be to do whatever it takes to save them. You would sooner risk your own life than risk losing them.

Do you see how our attitudes toward risk are subjective and dynamic? While our individual risk tolerance levels are a by-product of our personality types, our upbringings, culture, life experiences, and a whole host of other invisible forces, we have the ability to increase the amount of risk we are willing to incur depending upon our objectives.

What do you want to have more of in your life? Is it more money, more friends, more freedom, more fun? What would you be willing to risk to get it?

Whatever your age, if you want to become successful and begin leading a passion-filled life, it's not too late. I'm not saying it will be easy—you'll have to overcome your fears and everything else that is stopping you from going for your dreams.

The only certainty we have as we venture farther on our path in pursuit of our goals, is more uncertainty. Wouldn't certainty eventually bore you to death?

I'm challenging you to get out from under your covers and the safety of your sanctuary (whether you define that as your home or office). Set a big goal for yourself, something that is a stretch; be willing to take on some more risk and go for it.

You'll find that facing this challenge is exhilarating—even if it's scary and uncomfortable. You'll feel more alive as your blood starts coursing through your veins and your heart begins to pump harder. As your body's adrenaline kicks in, your breathing will increase, you may break a sweat, and your endorphins will give you such an incredible rush!

What are you waiting for?

Risk-taking is an essential component of my quality of life. Remaining a captive of self-limiting fear and playing it safe is unfulfilling (and not an option) for me.

I equate risk with challenge and understand it is a necessity of earning an associated reward. Each time I succeed in my efforts, I gain strength and greater confidence. The difficulties encountered along the way test my will, mold my character, and ultimately give me knowledge I wouldn't have learned in a book.

Of course it's foolish to take a risk just for the sake of it. A risk has to make sense. If the outcome of taking the risk is the achievement of a desirable objective (without hurting anyone or compromising my beliefs in the process), I'll most likely go for it.

It is risky to say, "I want to make a difference" as opposed to just going along and doing the things we do to be like everybody else.

It's risky to say, "I want more out of life," because people will be watching to see if you fail. And you will meet with obstacles that cause you to stumble along the way. But what is your alternative? Aren't you placing yourself at greater risk—in the grand scheme of things—by remaining complacent? When you want something to change and you don't speak up, who loses? You do.

What is the cost of living an unfulfilled life and failure to realize your potential? Would you want to see your children waste their lives and all opportunities for success and happiness by erring on the side of safety at all costs? Would you advise your children never to try out for a team, not to apply to the best school, or not to pursue the career or love of their life because there are associated risks? What kind of life would that be?

I'm encouraging you to take the risks that are consistent with where you want to be. I ask all of my financial planning and coaching clients to share with me where they want to be in three years. Try answering these questions for yourself right now:

1. Where do you want to be in three years? (Include as much detail as possible.)
2. Identify the top three obstacles that could prevent you from achieving those goals.
3. List all of the opportunities already present in your life that could help you to get to where you want to be in three years.
4. What personal strengths could you use to attain the life you want in three years?

Once you accept that taking risk is a prerequisite to living a passionate, successful life, you will start moving forward rather than allowing yourself to stay behind. There is no reward or joy in avoiding risk at all costs.

If you have faith in yourself and surround yourself with supportive people who want to see you succeed, you will find the answers and strength you need to persevere.

In closing, I want you to think about George Plimpton. Plimpton created a list of one hundred things he wanted to accomplish during his lifetime—all of which involved taking risks. He set out to fulfill as many things on the list as he could, and he led an extraordinary life.

I challenge you to make your own list of things to accomplish before you die. Start by striving to achieve the goals that involve small risks. Then stretch your list to include goals that require considerable risk and also the greatest rewards.

If you have what it takes to spend the rest of your days accomplishing each activity on your list, you will have an exhilarating and extraordinary life.

Exercises

1. Make a list of ten things you want to accomplish that require taking risks.
2. Write a story about a time when you took a risk and succeeded.
3. Write two stories about times when you took a risk and failed. Notice how failure impacts your current willingness to take the same risk.

For their inspiration and guidance with the material in this chapter, many thanks go to:

Steve Ferszt, Esq. For your intelligence and commitment to excellence.

Thomas Tyree, Jr. For leaving a prestigious investment bank to be a CFO and taking the company public.

Jocelyn Monroe. For doing triathlons and being a valuable member of my event planning team.

Melanie Dalyai. For marrying me in the face of prejudice.

Eric Yollick. For being a friend at Princeton who was clear about his political beliefs and willing to share them.

Wealthy Profile #8

Retired attorney and former city councilman, 72, married with a thirty-eight-year-old son, a thirty-six-year-old son, and four grandchildren. Lives in Queens, NY. He passed on his law practice to his eldest son and spends his time playing tennis, traveling, and supporting local Democrats. He is extremely humble and unassuming. He is involved with charitable pursuits that help inner-city children and Jewish causes. He feels his greatest accomplishment in life is his family. He is well-respected by both celebrities and civil servant workers because he treats everyone with honor. He worked very hard in areas where he could make a difference.

CHAPTER 13

Faith

Every wealthy person I have met possesses a strong sense of faith. These men and women who hail from different backgrounds—ethnicities, religions, social and economic classes—share the belief that everything in life eventually works out as it should.

This chapter contemplates the kind of faith that transcends any one religion. While some would question the wisdom of discussing faith in our current political environment, I think it would be a great disservice to omit a key ingredient of my personal recipe for leading a passion-filled, successful life.

In his book, *Care of the Soul*, Thomas More wrote, "Faith is a gift of spirit that allows the soul to remain attached to its own unfolding. When faith is soulful, it is always planted in the soil of wonder and questioning. It isn't a defensive and anxious holding on to certain objects of belief, because doubt, as its shadow, can be brought into a faith that is fully mature."

Let me clearly state for the record that I do not believe it is my place to tell you what to believe, what higher power to believe in, how to worship, or what is right or what is wrong. My objective is to share with you what works for me in terms of invaluable lessons and observations.

This chapter is grounded in philosophy and spirituality, not religion. I hope you will receive the messages presented herein with an open mind and heart.

My paternal grandmother Bernice was a Presbyterian who believed that preaching her faith was not about preaching her religion. She believed we must all practice what is preached in our churches, synagogues, and mosques.

My grandmother's deep faith had a profound influence on my life. I was blessed to have her love and guidance as a powerful force and active presence for so many years. If it were not for my grandmother's generosity and belief in me, I would not be where I am today. This book is a testament to the example she set for me to follow.

My father thinks my grandmother's greatest gift was her ability to see the good in everyone who crossed her path. She *looked* for the good in every single person she met. You see, in addition to my grandmother Bernice's faith in God, she believed divinity exists within every human soul.

When my grandmother addressed people, she focused on their goodness. When people did anything inconsistent with what a good person (she would say, "God person") would do, she wouldn't hesitate to tell them they had work to do.

When people she knew drank too much, abused drugs, skipped school, or you name it, she called them on it because she believed she knew who they really wanted to be. She was loved and respected by everyone who knew her, even though she could be quite critical and outspoken. People understood and appreciated that my grandmother always practiced constructive criticism.

Bernice died in 1998, at age 96. At her memorial service, the line of mourners literally extended outside the doors of her church. This one caring woman set so many people back onto their rightful paths by virtue of her faith. She prayed for every member of her family (and those she came to love as family) every day. She sought answers and genuinely felt that she received messages from God that were meant for the young people and adults in her life.

Even though it's been several years since Bernice passed away, by sharing the beliefs she had with all of us when she was alive, my grandmother made an impact on our lives that continues to serve us just as well today.

My grandmother introduced my father to the teachings of the late Eric But erworth, author of *Discover the Power Within You*. In his book, Butterworth wrote, "There is no such thing as a lack of faith. We all have plenty of faith; it's just that we have faith in the wrong things. We have faith in what can't be done rather than what can be done. We have faith in lack rather than abundance, but there is no lack of faith. Faith is a law."

Butterworth's devotees include people from all walks and stations of life, all of whom state that his teachings helped to change their lives. Dr. Maya Angelou said of Butterworth, "He has been, is now, and shall forever be my teacher."[1]

Oprah Winfrey credited this book with helping her to become who she is today. She said, "This book changed my perspective on life and religion. Eric Butterworth teaches that God isn't up there. He exists inside each one of us, and it's up to us to seek the divine within."[2]

Isn't that an incredibly empowering philosophy?

Inner strength can only be discovered once we call upon it. Until we seek it out, I think it resides quiet and dormant within the very core of our being. Spiritual people of all faiths rely upon this divine energy source—an inner voice—as a personal guidance system.

Even the most successful "self-made" people will tell you that they do not have all the answers. They need to find every answer just like everyone else. Much of their wisdom comes when they look inward. They have faith that "when the student is ready, the teacher will appear." They practice readiness and receptiveness; they actively ask questions and listen for answers.

The wealthiest people I've met always want to learn more and they have a wonderful curiosity about life. They believe messages and solutions are present all around us, so they have well-developed powers of observation.

It's up to each of us to find and receive the answers needed to achieve life's potential. If you don't have your eyes open, how will you see what's in front of you? If you don't turn the volume up, how will you hear your messages? While recognizing and receiving messages from your inner voice is essential to your ability to navigate in the direction of your goals, you'll also need to keep scanning your environment to pick up critical data and feedback from your friends, family, coworkers, and others you meet.

Once you learn how to activate your mind's "receiver," you'll notice solutions will seem to leap off the pages of the books, magazines, and newspapers you're reading, too. This will happen more and more as you get better at asking the right questions and your mind focuses on finding possible solutions—just as a computer sorts through volumes of data seeking matches to each query you put to it.

Have you ever noticed that when you are getting ready to buy a new car, you start seeing more of that type car everywhere you go? This is not a mystical phenomenon. It is a basic human cognitive function. Those cars were always all around you. But you didn't notice them because you weren't looking for them.

So start asking yourself questions about how you can achieve specific goals and let your mind take over. You must have faith that the answers you seek already exist around you. Some answers will take longer than others to become evident, but they will always come. Remember, it's up to you recognize your answers when they arrive.

Meditation has been a highly effective pathway for receiving answers to my questions. Just as my grandmother taught me how to pray, my father taught me how to meditate. My dad has practiced Transcendental Meditation for as long as I can remember.

How each of us chooses to tap into our source of higher intelligence will vary based on our religious upbringing, present spirituality, and openness. Many people only pray in a house of worship; others pray while driving the car or when they are at home kneeling at their bedside. Some people meditate in special classes or when practicing yoga; others prefer praying or meditating outdoors atop a secluded hill or by the water's edge.

Find what works for you, get still, and begin asking for the answers that will enable you to find your purpose and passions in life.

My grandmother taught me that we have the power to change our lives by altering our thoughts. I had faith in my grandmother and I practiced what she taught me, adapting my father's approach. This is what has worked for me.

I caution you not to take the powers of prayer and meditation lightly. You absolutely cannot do it while you are on the go (even if you are a consummate multi-tasker). This kind of deep reflection requires silence and zero distraction to achieve results.

At first, the hardest challenge you face will probably be finding quiet time. You must make the time. Some of my clients actually schedule their daily fifteen-minute period as an appointment on their personal calendars, in their appointment books, or PDAs. I tell clients to call this time, "My time for Me" and always suggest using a capital "M."

Quieting your mind and taking a time out from everything going on in the world around you requires tremendous discipline. If you have never learned how to center yourself, you may need to practice simply closing your eyes and keeping them closed, or noticing your breath and being with your breath.

Dedicate at least fifteen minutes every day to emptying your mind of worries, concerns, doubts, and upsets. I'm sure you're familiar with the phrase, "Let go, and let God." See if you can clear your mind long enough to fully experience the present moment.

Only when you've made it this far will you be able to hear the answers you're seeking and find the power you need to change your life. Until you can free your mind of unproductive thoughts, you won't be able to concentrate on new and empowering thoughts.

Whatever you do, don't give up. Keep trying, and you will achieve success. This journey to your spirit's source takes commitment and persistence.

When you are present in the moment, you will become conscious of the opportunities God is sending within each and every moment. Unfortunately, many people miss these precious moments when we are given infinite chances to grow, alter our destinies, and change the world as we know it.

While it may seem like a lot of work to learn how to find the answers you need to live a passionate life, do you consider your present life an acceptable alternative? If you do, more power to you. I'd rather self-actualize my soul than risk becoming a self-absorbed mess!

If you've had a vision for your life—a recurring dream of what you wish could be your reality—how do you think those thoughts got there? Is it possible that God gave you the ability to imagine something greater than what you have experienced, so you could strive to achieve that dream?

God wouldn't be so cruel as to tease us with the unattainable. If we desire a state of being that has come into our awareness, then we are given an abundance of answers and resources to achieve it. The onus is on us to be paying attention.

The universal desire to achieve our hopes and dreams lies within each of our hearts. Each of us has to take responsibility for whether we live our dreams or die without achieving them. No one can live our lives for us—there are some places we must go alone.

When you look into your heart for answers and strength, spend some time telling yourself you deserve happiness and love. Look for the divine goodness that is already inside of you (just as my grandmother would).

If you don't have faith in yourself, is it fair to expect anyone else to have faith in you or your vision? When I ask myself this question, I think of Ted Turner.

Do you think Turner would have been able to launch Cable News Network (CNN) if he didn't believe in himself and his vision? Would Turner have succeeded in getting others to participate in building his superstation if he lacked confidence in his idea? Could he have withstood losing $900 million before his vision for CNN was realized if he didn't have faith in himself?

As I see it, Turner had to have an unwavering faith in what he was creating. He had to believe in himself and his ability to bring his vision into reality. Even though he had a dream and the resources he needed to build the network that changed the world, it wasn't a slam-dunk.

Ted Turner has the mindset of a champion. As a man who has the wealth to acquire anything he wants, he knows better than most anyone else that the things truly worth having in life don't come easy. Turner is a man who thrives on overcoming challenges.

Can you imagine where this nation and world would be if

more people had Ted Turner's attitude and drive? Unfortunately, too many of the men and women I meet within the confines of corporate America fail because they mistakenly believe their lives are harder than most. Often, when sharing philosophies about life and success, people complain about all of the obstacles they believe prevent them from becoming successful. They don't understand that there is only one real obstacle they must learn to overcome—their own belief system.

It is a fatal error in thinking to believe our lives would be so much better if only we had it easier. The true test of character is how one deals with adversity. Failures, disasters, and setbacks, are all incredible learning and growth opportunities in disguise.

When you meet with crisis or any situation that "tests your faith," why not choose to see it as a test of what you're made of? It is no less than thrilling when we call upon our inner strength and resources to find a solution and prevail.

In many cases there will be no precedence for the solutions we come upon. Albert Einstein said, "We can't solve problems by using the same kind of thinking we used when we created them." We have to go to a different level of thinking, a different level of being, and a different level of trust and faith to arrive at many of the solutions we will need to succeed in life.

If you avoid being challenged, you will stop growing. That is no way to live. Holding yourself hostage to your fears is counter to the mindset of a champion and the passion for success. Faith is an omnipotent ally you must nurture.

Do you believe there is a silver lining in every cloud? Do you look for the rainbow after every rainstorm? I do. I am an unapologetic optimist. While I see life's dangers and problems as clearly as any pessimist, my faith in all things ultimately working out carries me through life. If I genuinely believed nothing I do can make a difference and that my efforts will result in failure, what would be my incentive to try?

It's ironic that many of the pessimists I meet proclaim they are "realists." As I see it, these individuals have come to their viewpoint by meeting with failure early in life and allowing their experience to serve as an excuse for not achieving anything truly worthwhile.

Many of these same personality types believe the world owes them something rather than the other way around. These sorry souls wander through life aimlessly and often follow leaders who promise them something for nothing. But there is no such thing!

Don't be led by false prophets or profits. Please do not fall into the trap of "blind faith." After Enron, faithful employees around the world found their "faith" was shattered. Some may have asked God how this could happen, but they put their trust in the wrong leaders. (Shouldn't we be asking instead how we can prevent these types of violations of trust from happening again? The Enron crisis was tragic and it served as a wake-up call—an opportunity for us all to learn and grow. For one thing, maybe we needed to be reminded to take more personal responsibility for our well-being and retirement.)

Many people tell me they've been let down by their companies, bosses, coworkers, institutions, parents, and friends. I am not suggesting that you "trust no one." Faith is about trust. But having faith doesn't mean you need to check your brains at the door.

The people we meet in life should earn our trust over time. You need to be smart. You need to figure out whom to go to for what. And there may be instances when someone betrays your trust and you need to go your separate ways.

We all must discern for ourselves who is worthy of our trust and who is not. While I maintain that everyone we meet on our path has arrived to teach us lessons we need to learn, be cognizant that some of our teachers will show us the darker sides of life.

Not all teachers will be sweet, loving, kind, and innocent. They're not supposed to be. I've learned how to deal with life's challenges from my grandmother and from a bully in school. In each case, they taught me lessons necessary for my growth and development.

To go through life without any sense of direction would be a wasted life. God has put me on this planet for a reason. I want to do my part to leave things better than they were when I arrived.

In my own life, I keep watching and listening for the messages I need so I can learn and become the "God person" my grandmother believed I could become. If I create a clear vision of where I am to go—as long as it serves the greater good—everything in my world will align itself with that vision.

So the final question is, is there an absolute truth or is it all open to our individual interpretation? Since I believe we are born with the power to create infinite possibilities, I don't believe in an absolute. Before Roger Bannister, people thought it was humanly impossible to run a mile in less than four minutes. In 1954, Bannister changed our understanding of what is possible.

Each day I go within myself and trust the messages I need to receive will come from the Holy Spirit. I believe miracles (which I define as completely unexpected and welcome) occur every day.

I invite you to take my hand and jump off the high diving board of life with me. Let's take an exhilarating leap of faith into the glorious unknown of our days ahead and find wonder in the miracles we witness in every moment along the way.

Exercises

1. Write a list of specific actions you will take to incorporate faith in your daily life.
2. Ask your religious advisor to share a story of how faith makes a positive impact in someone's life.
3. Develop your own positive, self-affirming statement, such as "I am in the flow of life, and everything is possible because I have faith." Close your eyes and repeat it at least once a day.

For their inspiration and guidance with the material in this chapter, many thanks go to:

Eric Butterworth. For your metaphysical teachings and belief in my inner self.

Rich DeVos. For introducing me to great motivational speakers and books.

Bernard Silverman. For sharing your knowledge of Judaism through our *HaTanakh*.

Charlie Ward. For sharing your strong belief in God as we gave you financial guidance.

Cheryl Johnson. For being a spiritual support in my personal development, which began when we met at Princeton.

CHAPTER 14

Empowerment

Y ou were born with the potential to better yourself, your life, and the world around you. Once you get your inner "mojo" flowing again, nothing can stop you. As your awareness expands, so will your ability to access everything needed to sustain your efforts to build the life you imagine for yourself.

My personal vision for *The Passion for Success* is to stimulate your thoughts and stir up the desire within you to act on the ideas presented herein. If you take the initiative to follow through, you will succeed.

My grandmother's faith in every person lives on inside of me and on the pages of this book. Bernice understood she couldn't live my life for me. She relied on her faith in me to inspire, guide, and empower me. One of her greatest gifts was teaching me self-reliance by always making sure I aimed high and constantly encouraging me to be the best person I could be.

For me, empowerment is a "guided letting go," rather than doing things for others that they need to do for themselves. Do not make the mistake of trying to do anyone else's work for them—whether it's your kids' homework, a co-worker's job, or a family member's addiction. If you do fall into that trap, you unwittingly create a cycle of dependence.

It is often painful to see the ones you love having a hard time, but it's in the struggle that they find their own power to grow. If you don't think the people in your life have the ability to overcome whatever difficulties they may encounter on their path, then you lack faith. This is your problem—don't make it theirs!

Empowerment teaches people to believe in (and tap into) their own greatness. I resent the legacy of the misguided efforts of "limousine liberals" who through their charity have contributed to the disempowerment of entire families living on the lowest rungs of our nation's socio-economic ladder.

So many wealthy individuals have their hearts in the right place, but we need to understand that throwing money at other people's problems only enables their problems. To bring about real change, we should also offer our support through words and actions that help those people to help themselves.

I vehemently disagree with the Reverend Jesse Jackson's fight for reparations for the descendants of African American slaves, because coexisting in this symbolic gesture is the message that we can't overcome our past. That is bunk.

If we want to change our collective self-image, we need to reaffirm the message that all of us are born with the seeds of greatness firmly planted in our core. Each of us has the ability to triumph over every disadvantage (past and present).

Look at Oprah Winfrey. Where would that woman be if she bought into an attitude of entitlement? If Oprah had allowed others to take away her personal power by accepting their well-meaning welfare, this world would be without an extraordinary leader who continues to set an example for all of us to follow.

Oprah's philanthropy doesn't end with her signature on a check. This dynamic billionaire is tireless in her personal efforts to bring about change—whether it's in the poorest neighborhoods in Chicago or the starving villages of Africa. She is a highly visible proponent of education because she understands its role in personal empowerment.

Teaching your children, friends, or family how to do their own research to find the resources that will provide them the knowledge and skills to accomplish their objectives in life is a magnificent gift. When we teach people where to find the tools they require to make it in life (and how to use them), we are actually giving them something far more valuable, potent, and lasting than money by itself.

These days, many adults are stressed out because they feel they are always running short of time, and their lack of patience often results in taking counterproductive shortcuts. It always seems easier to give an inquiring child a quick answer and more expedient to do a new employee's task for them. Yet it would only take a little more time at that moment if you guided people to figure things out for themselves. By showing others how to think for themselves, you foster their independence and they become less dependent on you and your time.

Our law schools commonly utilize the interactive Socratic method of teaching to develop their students' critical thinking skills. Rather than providing lists of answers to memorize and spit back, instructors ask questions designed to stimulate learning. Isn't it better to teach someone how to think than to provide the answer key? What's the point of having the answers if we don't know how to apply them to our lives?

You wouldn't believe how many times parents have told me they have to get home to do homework with their kids. I'm not talking about conversing with their kids in a foreign language or making up an earth science experiment to supplement their child's classroom assignments. Educated, affluent, well-meaning parents actually *do* their kids' homework for them. I don't ever remember my mother or father doing homework with me, or any of my friends having their parents do homework with them. Do you?

What are these parents hoping to accomplish? If they think giving their children the answers to their homework assignments will help get them the grades needed to get into an exclusive prep school or an Ivy League college, what do they expect will happen once their kids are on their own and have to begin thinking for themselves?

Many parents don't even let go when their kids go to college. Recent television and newspaper reports have documented accounts of overanxious parents calling their children to wake them for class and arriving on campus to handle problems with faculty and administration.

These really nice moms and dads are inadvertently harming their children for life! Doing your child's homework (or any other type of work, for that matter) is dysfunctional. One of the greatest lessons you can teach your children is that they have the intelligence and talent to find the answers they will need wherever they go in life.

Besides, don't you enjoy the feeling of satisfaction that comes from figuring out the answer to a difficult question? Why deprive your children of experiencing those same feelings?

I love the thrill of overcoming a challenge. Whenever I solve a problem, I gain in my level of self-confidence. The more we do for ourselves and increase our competencies in every aspect of our lives, the more we benefit from greater confidence and self-esteem.

We need to keep our eyes firmly focused on the end goal, which is to empower our children to succeed when they go out into the world. Sometimes failing or getting a "B" will teach them more about the kind of effort required to succeed in life than getting an "A."

How do you expect our young adults to survive in the business world today when the Internet makes it possible for billions of kids living in Canada, South America, Eastern Europe, Asia, and India to compete for the same jobs? If we want them to stand a chance at being self-sufficient (and eventually leave home), we've got to expose them to increasingly greater challenges and competition throughout their development.

The owner of a tutoring service, a woman received a call from a mother who complained that one of the staff tutors was upsetting this woman's daughter. When my friend asked the client to please tell her what happened, she replied that "the tutor is making my daughter do too much work."

Would this woman's daughter stand a chance if she had to compete against some of the immigrant children coming to our high schools from Asia and Russia? Probably not. I don't say this because I believe the daughter lacks ability. It's her mom's attitude that is all wrong.

I've also heard some of the parents in an affluent suburb of New York City say it's not fair that their kids have to compete against "the Asian kids" (because the Asian students in their high schools are consistently ranking at the top of their classes). The school now has a bell curve for the Asian students and one for everyone else. People's attitudes have gotten so out of hand— if you didn't know better, you might think these immigrant kids had landed from another planet and had been endowed with super-human abilities! Is it too much of a stretch that these new Americans are simply working harder than their classmates who hail from second- and third-generation American families?

Why do you think such a disproportionate number of young leaders tend to be born to immigrant families? The answer is so simple: their parents expect more from them than do many of the established middle- and upper-class American families who have grown too comfortable and complacent enjoying an easier life.

Do athletes with serious Olympic aspirations ask their coaches to make their drills easier? If my goal is to improve the level of my tennis game, would I want my instructor to keep hitting easy shots to me? Of course not!

The standard of living and pace at which our lives are evolving seem to be increasing at an exponential rate. Athletes today have to run faster, be stronger, and compete at higher levels than the generations that came before them.

Let's stop with all this catering to people, guiltily giving handouts to the poor, and feeling sorry for them. That's the worst thing you can do for people, because you take away their power. Learn to look for the greatness in every person you meet.

When your kids or grandkids come to you for answers, tell them how much you love them. But don't stop there. Tell them how smart you think they are and how much faith you have in their ability to find the answers on their own. They'll thank you—when they grow up!

If you meet someone who asks for your help, ask him or her, "Where do you want to go with your life? In an ideal world, where do you see yourself in three years?" Encourage them to put themselves out there and dream big. Also ask them, "What are the top three obstacles that are going to prevent you from getting there?" You may be surprised by the honest replies people will give you. Most people are painfully aware of their circumstances as well as what's preventing them from living the life they want to have. They don't need you or me to tell them. What they do need is someone who can offer hope, encouragement, support, friendship, and faith in their abilities. They, just like you, must discover inner strength and take the actions that will allow them to achieve their goals and aspirations.

Because I have reconnected to my own source of inner strength, I'll meet people who ask me how I've done it. I'm happy to share with them the steps I've taken to become the person I am today, as well as the actions I am taking to become the man I want to be tomorrow.

Sometimes I think of empowerment as charging someone else's battery. Some days all it takes is a conversation to feel charged. In some cases, more time and energy must be expended to boost someone's battery. Just be careful not to let negative people drain you of your positive energies. It may take practice to learn when to let go of those people.

At work, we should expect to give our coworkers or employees what is required for them to perform their jobs, in both resources and motivation. Then it's important to get out of the way and see what they can do.

Experienced leaders understand that empowerment is letting others rise to the occasion; it's not about doing for others. Empowerment encourages people to take the initiative and see for themselves that they have the right stuff.

On the other hand, if an employee doesn't want to do the work required as a condition for employment, or if your kids don't want to do their homework after you've advised them of the consequences of their inaction, then let them make their own choices. There will be many times when people close to us suffer harsh penalties as a result of personal choices. But respecting every individual's freedom to make his or her own decisions is essential to empowerment.

As the old adage says, "You can lead a horse to water, but you can't make it drink." If the horse doesn't want to take a sip of that clean refreshing water, accept it! When the horse gets thirsty, he'll start drinking the water.

The majority of people you know are probably intelligent and most likely will do what is necessary to avoid pain. We all certainly understand that it's human nature to decline well-intended advice at times. Eventually, we learn the lessons we need to learn. That said, have more faith in your kids, friends, lovers, and teammates, and do your part to empower them.

If your parents failed to empower you because of their own

issues, you must come to terms with this unfortunate reality and find the resources (both internally and externally) to empower yourself. Some of the men and women I meet tell me they are grateful for a grandmother, an aunt, an uncle, an older sibling, a friend's parent, or a teacher who believed in them and encouraged them throughout their early life.

My mother, Minnette (Mindy) Eaton, was so generous of spirit and the most selfless person I have ever known. She devoted herself to her three sons, loving and empowering us on so many levels. She had so much love and good energy that it seemed she attracted every child in the neighborhood to our house on some days.

If you had been lucky enough to meet my mother, you never would have known she was without the benefit of love and nurturing from her own mother. My mom's wisdom, in its entirety, came from her desire to become the antithesis of what she saw in her parents.

She liked to tell us that we filled her up with so much pride. And, since that made us feel so good, we would do whatever we could to always make her feel proud of us. It became a never-ending cycle of empowerment.

Ultimately, when the cycle of empowerment comes full circle, you will feel the tremendous impact your love and support has had on others, because it will come back to you.

Exercises

1. Go to the local college and offer your services to mentor a student who is interested in your field. Meet with the student at least once a month.
2. Ask the most successful person in your field to be your mentor and guide your development.
3. Visit a person in need and listen to what he or she wants in life.

For their inspiration and guidance with the material in this chapter, many thanks go to:

Betty Bracey. For being my fifth grade teacher and my favorite educator.

Anthony Robbins. For your commitment to creating an extraordinary life for all.

Jeffery Weaver. For being my greatest advocate in my financial planning business.

Steve Siegel. For being a role model for commercial real estate professionals.

Jami Beere. For always connecting people in mutually beneficial relationships.

CHAPTER 15

Circle of Success

Five years from now you will be the person you are becoming based on the people with whom you associate, the books you read, and the choices you make. To understand how much weight the first part of that equation carries, if I met the five closest people in your life right now, I would know the person you will be with a high degree of certainty.

Many of the parents I meet realize the power of influence friends have on their children's development and, ultimately, their success. This is one of the reasons why so much emphasis is placed on what schools children attend. So why not apply this same rationale in our own lives? Shouldn't we be just as vigilant about the company we keep?

In Florida, I meet many couples in their sixties, seventies, and eighties who live in retirement communities with hundreds of other "seniors." Too often their conversations revolve around doctor appointments, the status of a terminally ill neighbor, complaints about kids who don't call or visit, and worries about money.

If you notice this kind of thinking and relating has taken root within your circle of friends, please don't brush it off as trivial. It's not. Negative thinking is like a fast-growing cancer. Protect yourself against its effects as if your life depends on it. Don't excuse it as part of getting old. Not all retirees think alike.

If your peer group has accepted diabetes, osteoporosis, and poor heart or muscle function as status quo, I urge you to find new friends. As a wise person once said, "If you hang with the lame, you'll begin to limp!" (Of course, I am speaking to an attitude and not suggesting you abandon a sick friend.)

How many of your friends are physically active? Do you

know any coworkers, family members, or friends who are disciplined with their diet, exercise, and commitment to a healthy lifestyle?

At my gym, there is a woman in her sixties who works out for two to three hours just about every day. She has better muscle tone than almost anyone I've ever met. This dynamic woman is creating a new career for herself as a fitness model.

Look at the people with whom you spend most of your time. Consider where they are in life, in terms of their:

- Overall health and fitness
- Education
- Financial success
- Spiritual development
- Interest in philanthropy
- Closeness to family
- Friendships
- Passion for success

Your findings will give you a good indication as to where *you* will be five years from now (if your present relationships remain unchanged).

Each of us has complete control over whom we choose to spend our time with each day. Most of us choose friends and coworkers who are at our present level of development because doing so provides us with a level of comfort and a sense of familiarity. We tend to like people who are like ourselves.

If you want to grow and strengthen your life's weaker aspects, surround yourself with people who are strong and successful in those areas. Spend as much time with them (as is sensible) on a regular basis. Let me share an example of how I applied this thinking to my business life:

My former business partner was very astute and responsible in handling our firm's finances. I credit him with helping me to increase my annual income by ten-fold in part because I started to take on the practices he incorporated in his daily life. But, initially, there was some pain associated with being around someone who did things so differently to how I had always done them.

When it came to our expenses, he focused on every single expense we incurred—lunches, dinners, office paper, copier costs, staff salaries, and bonuses—all those "little details" I had always tended to trivialize. He'd ask for every credit card receipt for every charge I made in order to determine if we were charged the proper amount for each line item on every billing statement. This man was my role model for financial accountability.

Although we parted ways, I am grateful to my former partner's influence on me. He helped me to become more aware of my business expenses and spending decisions. Now I have incorporated many of his thorough approaches into my thinking and daily business practices.

Sometimes, even after we've learned a better way of managing an area of our lives, we return to our comfort level and normal approach. That has happened to me in certain areas of my business life. Going back to some of my old ways cost me a lot of money.

I made the mistake of thinking I could handle everything, but my confidence in my ability to be disciplined and take on all the things my partner once handled was a bit premature.

If this happens to you, know that all is not lost (as long as you catch yourself in time). My experience taught me the value of creating my personal support infrastructure to provide the consistent reinforcement I needed to stay on course.

The network of people in my Circle of Success is what I affectionately refer to as my personal "Board of Directors." We don't actually meet as a group, but I do make a point of staying in regular contact with each member of my support team.

Let me explain more about how to create your Circle of Success. Once you have identified an area of your personal or professional life you want to strengthen, seek out a qualified "expert" in your network who is willing to serve as your coach.

For example, if you determine you have a need to strengthen yourself in the area of spiritual development, a likely candidate for the role of your spiritual coach may be your minister, or a close friend. For help with my spiritual development, I look for people who are also giving by nature and make a habit of helping others.

Before requesting guidance from a particular individual, think about how well his or her overall values and attitudes agree with your own. If you are more liberal by nature, it probably wouldn't be wise to seek the support of someone who is very conservative (or vice versa).

If you are wondering how you might approach someone to become part of your Circle of Success, remind yourself that the success-oriented have an innate desire to make a difference in the world. When you ask someone to give of themselves for this purpose, you are acknowledging his or her importance and ability to effect change in your life. Most people will be more than willing to help and will consider your request a tremendous compliment. Wouldn't you feel great if you were asked to serve as someone's mentor?

Now let's say you are trying to improve your overall fitness and physical appearance. Doesn't it make sense to go to the fittest people you know and ask them how they stay fit? When I asked one young woman at my gym how she keeps herself in such great shape, she was flattered and happy to tell me about her regimen. She said, "I work out every day. I watch what I eat, I do Yoga and meditate. I make it a must in my life to exercise every day."

It's that simple to get answers to your questions about how to improve your life. Actually putting those actions into regular practice is where difficulties arise. This is why it's so important for you to cultivate an ongoing relationship specific to your goals with each member of your Circle of Success.

Until each new skill set you are working to develop is solidly in place in your life, you should stay in close contact with your success mentors. You will find that your Circle of Success relationships serve to keep you on track as you work toward the attainment of each goal.

Tony Gordon has made the Top of the Table in the life insurance industry twenty-seven consecutive times. He earns more than a million dollars a year selling life insurance! While almost anyone can have a good year if they land a big account, to do so twenty-seven times puts Tony in a different league. In my mind, he is someone I can learn from.

Tony is focused on producing results, skilled at listening, manages his staff well, and models himself after people who are two or three levels above him. He looks to some of his clients to teach him success habits he can incorporate into his professional life.

One member of Tony's Circle of Success is a multi-millionaire who makes a list of the things he will accomplish for the day. When Tony asked him what happens if he doesn't accomplish everything on the list, his client said, "I do not call the day complete until that list is complete."

Talk about leaving no wiggle room—what a concept! Most of us fail to keep a resolution the moment we give ourselves some wiggle room. Successful people honor their commitments.

If you ordered a new car, how would you feel if you were promised delivery for Saturday and then receive a call telling you it won't come in for another week? Do you think the car dealer should allow wiggle room on this commitment? Doesn't it tick you off when someone breaks a commitment to you? Do you think it's acceptable to break the commitments you make to yourself?

Even with our own Circle of Success in place, we are still responsible for our actions as well as our failure to take action. Remember, the only person staring back at you in the mirror at the end of the day is you. How you feel when you look yourself in the eye will depend upon whether or not you've honored your commitments.

The people we invite into our Circle can add a dimension of external pressure to supplement our personal resolve as we work toward attaining particular goals. To illustrate the value of enlisting the help of others, consider the reasons why so many people hire personal trainers. At first, you may rely upon the trainer to teach you how to use the equipment in the gym and guide you as you develop the right techniques for lifting weights, etc. But once you've acquired basic knowledge and have a prescribed exercise plan to get you to your desired weight and muscle mass, what's the benefit of continuing with the trainer?

For many people, a personal trainer is more than a teacher. Their trainers also serve as very important persons to meet at an appointed time and place. It's too easy to break a date with yourself; it's much harder to break our dates with others. Also, let's be honest, it can be tempting to take shortcuts when no one is looking. Trainers don't allow us to cheat during their watch.

The people who stand by us and keep us company as we travel on the road to personal growth are wonderful sources of moral support. This is apparent when the going gets tough and we are tempted to give up.

Imagine you've told a friend you're not eating dessert until you lose ten pounds. And you've asked for your friend's support as you work toward this goal. If you order that triple chocolate layer cake one week into your diet when you are dining with your friend, he'll call you on it because that's the agreement you made.

I am more likely to achieve certain goals when I employ the Beatles' adage to get "a little help from my friends," than when I try to go the distance alone. Even if you are fortunate to be endowed with tremendous talent and drive, there is no substitute for the impact external feedback can have on your ability to attain higher levels of performance.

How does a top athlete sustain the motivation required to improve without any competitor on the horizon? No one would argue Michael Jordan's greatness on the basketball court. So how could Jordan's coach, Phil Jackson (who never reached Jordan's level of play), help the champion get even better? One answer is that Jackson saw his player's potential to step it up, and was able to supplement Jordan's inner motivation.

This goes back to faith and empowerment. The player-coach relationship is a beautiful collaboration because the athlete continues to reach within to play the game the coach knows is possible.

Some might compare a coach to an army drill instructor. Whether the task is coaching athletes or training soldiers, the aim is the same: help people be the best that they can be.

Business coaches and industry study groups are common ways success-minded executives and entrepreneurs employ the

Circle of Success concept. If you are seeking a management consultant or "Master Mind" group to join for added support and guidance as you grow your business, be sure to approach those who have achieved success one or two levels above where you are now.

Going back to a tennis analogy, if my goal is to get better, I need to work with a coach or hit with players who will raise my level of play. Avoid the temptation to be content.

It is easier to get trapped when we are standing still, especially when we are surrounded by a peer group of equal or lesser abilities. Corporate America harbors far too many people who prefer to associate with others who are less proficient, intelligent, and driven than themselves. This seems counterintuitive until you realize their goal isn't to be the best at what they do. The true objective of these corporate-types is to *appear* better than everyone else. There is a world of difference between this kind of thinking and the mindset of a champion.

The real success stories in corporate America are the executives and entrepreneurs who possess the passion for success. These men and women seek out others who are more intelligent, more ambitious, more street smart, more driven, and more polished than themselves. The Circles of Success they create are meant to keep these achievers humble and on their toes.

When I ask people to become part of my Circle of Success, I look for those who I'd really like to spend my time getting to know. Also, I discreetly determine how potential candidates for my Circle have arrived at where they are in life. Someone who has inherited wealth or title may not be able to give me the insight I need to create my own step-by-step process for becoming a multi-millionaire.

If you're on your way up, you want to look for the people who went before you, struggled as you will, and figured out effective ways to get from here to there. In fact, people who have failed on their way to becoming successful are the best teachers in the world. They can also help you succeed quicker because their experience can save you a lot of trial and error.

Some of the qualifying questions I may ask a prospective Circle of Success member include:

- How do you define success?
- Do you see yourself as successful?
- How did you get started in your career?
- What was your ultimate goal?
- How did you achieve your success?
- What daily practices do you consider essential for your continued success?
- Are you happy?
- How do you define happiness?
- If you could do your life over again, what would you do differently?
- What is your greatest accomplishment in life?

Of course the actual questions I ask are tailored to the individual and what type of support I'm seeking.

Your objective is to learn how the other person thinks and how well he can communicate his insights. Whatever you do, stay clear of people who don't practice what they preach and people who make it easy for you to continue with your bad habits.

If an alcoholic wanted to quit drinking, it certainly wouldn't make sense to hang out in bars with friends who are still drinking. If you wanted to hire a personal trainer to help you reach your fitness goals, you'll get better results with someone who serves as a role model by possessing the physical fitness and mental toughness you want to acquire. A mentor must have the know-how and lead by example. Do you think you'd get the same result from an out-of-shape trainer as you would from the leanest, toughest trainer in town?

Go to the people who make you feel uncomfortable about staying where you are in life. Again, if you want to get in shape, find people who set a higher standard in terms of what they eat, their workout habits, and how they take care of themselves.

Do not make the common mistake of thinking you can find one superhuman person to be your ultimate "success guru." The reason we all need a Circle of Success is because no one person is a master of everything. The person who becomes your fitness role model may not be a wise choice to offer you financial advice.

Remember these words: If it's to be, it's up to me! Don't lose sight of the purpose for your Circle of Success. It's to provide you with support in the form of mentors and role models who set the standards for success in each area of your life. It's up to you to do the work needed to realize each and every goal you set.

I teach myself by asking each member of my Circle of Success the right questions, and I observe their practices. I know it's my job to:

- Ask the probing questions
- Spend time with every great person who joins my Circle
- Analyze my role models' actions regularly
- Put what I learn into action in my own life

Our most valuable lessons in life are learned through our experiences with others. If you respect others and see the greatness they possess, you can learn a lot from them.

Surround yourself with a Circle of Success consisting of people who have succeeded in the specific facets of life in which you aspire to shine brighter.

When you begin to mirror the practices they have incorporated in their own lives, you'll start to see a change in how you appear in your mirror each night. When you read the books your success mentors are reading, attend the classes they are attending, and take the risks they are taking, you will experience a more extraordinary life than if you tried to do it all by yourself.

Be willing to be uncomfortable around greatness because that's how you shall become great. If your heart doesn't start pumping harder and you don't break a sweat in your new Circle, you haven't reached high enough.

Never stop searching for new people to join your support team. Some of the people in your Circle today won't be in your Circle tomorrow. As long as you keep changing and growing, so will your inner Circle.

Above all, acknowledge and thank each and every person who contributes to your success along the way. Remember there is no such thing as a totally self-made man or woman.

Exercises

1. Using the questions on page 164, interview three prospective members of your inner circle about their financial success.
2. Repeat #1 for your spiritual Circle of Success.
3. Repeat #1 for your physical Circle of Success.

For their inspiration and guidance with the material in this chapter, many thanks go to:

Rob McGrath. For believing in me and being a financial partner in my vision.

Gary Joyal. For sharing your business acumen while we exercise at the Athletic Club Boca Raton.

Jeffrey Lowin. For offering an office while I was creating Eaton Life.

Kenneth Grosso. For being someone who takes action immediately to produce results.

Arthur Backal. For being someone who attracts the most affluent people in New York and for planning all of their special events

CHAPTER 16

Acknowledgment

Don't skip this chapter! If you read the title again you will notice there is no *s* at the end of *Acknowledgment*. This is not the part of the book you usually see at the beginning—the section where the author thanks mom, dad, teachers, friends, et al. Perhaps after reading this chapter you will understand why those acknowledgments exist and why they are so important.

Acknowledgment is about recognition. I actively *acknowledge* others each and every day of my life. This is no exaggeration; if you ask anyone who knows me, they will tell you so.

I look for something good, or a certain unique quality, in every person I meet. Then I make it a point to acknowledge what I've observed by looking the person in the eye and explicitly saying what I noticed.

Acknowledgment is an extension of my grandmother's faith in the god-ness within all of us. As I explained back in chapter 13, Bernice looked for the good qualities in every person she met. By sharing her observations, she empowered people.

Let's be careful to distinguish between acknowledgment and flattery. *Flattery* is false praise. Telling a noticeably out-of-shape person you think they're looking incredibly fit isn't acknowledgment—it's a lie! It is completely appropriate to acknowledge the difference you see in someone who has lost twenty pounds.

Every time we acknowledge an individual's special quality or good deed, we make a direct deposit into his or her empowerment fund. Serving as a source of positive feedback for other people adds real value to their lives. The deposits my grandmother made into my emotional empowerment account continue to earn compound interest today!

When you make a regular practice of expressing admiration, gratitude, and praise, you will become the kind of person others want to be around. All of us naturally want to surround ourselves with genuine people who make us feel good. We need to hear positive reinforcement more than criticism because there's always more than enough of the negative stuff to go around.

Make no mistake: I am not a fan of brownnosers or sycophants. Insincerity is such a turnoff. In fact, when you agree to your boss' bad idea or offer false praise with the motivation of gaining favor, you do more harm than good.

Honest, healthy, constructive feedback is essential to every authentic relationship. So is telling people when they've done a good job, thanking them when they've made your day better, and catching them in the act of doing something right. I'm suggesting you put some of your powers of observation to good use by "accentuating the positive" as the old Johnny Mercer-Harold Arlen song advised.

If looking for the positive in people doesn't come naturally to you, invest your time and energy on cultivating this interpersonal skill. At first, you might find it helpful to make a game of developing your acknowledgment abilities when you are in various social settings. The object of acknowledgment is to notice something positive about at least one person you speak with at each event. You do not win any points unless you share your observation with the person directly. You gain a point for each person you acknowledge with a sincere compliment.

It really feels good to make someone else feel good. I get such a thrill out of making someone else's day simply by sharing what I've noticed—which usually elicits a smile and leaves that individual happier than before we had the opportunity of engaging in even the briefest of conversations.

There are many ways to practice acknowledgment. The most meaningful acknowledgments I remember receiving were on my fortieth birthday.

To celebrate the big day, I hosted a special party and invited one hundred people who had made a significant difference in my life. Along with the invitation, party guests received an RSVP card and self-addressed stamped envelope to return, indicating whether or not they could attend. What was unusual about the card was the additional request for a brief note describing how I had made a difference in that person's life.

I admit this may sound a bit unorthodox, but this was only the first half of the acknowledgment. On the day of my party, each of my guests received a handwritten note from me, too. In each acknowledgment I shared my gratitude for something special that individual had said or done that affected my life.

You would not believe what kind of reaction and feelings these acknowledgments generated.

One of the wonderful things about a written acknowledgment is its permanence. Many people cherish the words of appreciation we write in notes so much so that they hold onto your words to read again and again.

Acknowledgment doesn't always have to be so deep or dramatic. Whenever I see a beautiful tie, I can't resist asking about it. And when I've said, "Wow, what a great tie—where did you get it?" even the most powerful and reserved men will usually respond by telling me the details of the occasion when a special person gave it to them. Often, I've ended up enjoying conversations with some very interesting and accomplished individuals (even at the stuffiest of affairs) by virtue of offering a friendly compliment.

Why do so many beautiful women rarely hear any acknowledgment of how great they look except from guys who hit on them? The shame of it is that their beauty intimidates other women and many men. The same attitude toward very successful men and women seems to hold true. Even they need to hear that their hair looks nice, their outfit or shoes are stunning, or they have a wonderful smile.

Many of the people I speak with at my seminars find it intimidating to approach someone who is more attractive or successful than they are. If you share this mindset, I urge you to make a commitment to work on improving your self-esteem.

Every human being craves acknowledgment, whether it's a pat on the back, a kind word, or a thank you. Don't make the mistake of thinking that people who are rich, famous, or beautiful don't need to hear compliments, and don't discount the value of offering your appreciation when you have the opportunity to meet an individual you admire.

It's almost comical to see how grown men and women act when they meet celebrities. If your goal at a fundraising function is only to impress a famous stranger, don't waste your time. It is always so awkward to watch a bunch of guys trying to act cool when they corner a professional athlete for a conversation. I'm suggesting that you approach the guest of honor and express how much you appreciate his or her involvement in a particular cause and why this is so important to you. Your brief exchange makes a lasting impact on that VIP's life because you'll convey the message that this person is truly making a difference in your life.

A good friend of mine actually researches the background of the prominent people with whom she may be doing business before they meet. By taking the time to learn what she can about these successful men and women, she sets herself apart in their minds as someone who is genuinely interested in relating to them at a different level than her competitors. She never fails to make a good impression. She understands that acknowledgment enables others to feel good (no matter who they are). They in turn view her as someone who sees her own connection to the bigger picture or shared goal.

Acknowledgment also needs to come from the top down. In Jack Welch's best-selling autobiography, *Straight from the Gut*, the former CEO of General Electric underscores the importance of acknowledging each person's contribution to the company's success. Welch said it was hard for him to think in terms of what he as an individual accomplished at GE, because he understood that the company's success was the result of each employee's unique contribution.

I meet too many managers and owners of firms who tell me they don't acknowledge their employees because they don't want the employees to become too comfortable! In some cases, when people withhold praise and appreciation, they fear appearing less powerful to their subordinates. Nothing could be further from the truth! When we empower others with words of acknowledgment, we tap into a wellspring of power that resides at the highest spiritual level.

People often tell me they don't want to approach a member of the opposite sex with an acknowledgment for fear their innocent remarks may be mistaken for what our parents' generation referred to as "making a pass." If you are married or in a committed relationship, that doesn't mean you have to stop acknowledging the opposite sex. Acknowledge responsibly!

If you clearly let the person you're talking with know you are married or are in a relationship upfront, there is no reason on earth why you can't say something positive to members of the opposite sex. In fact, your kind words will be appreciated even more when they realize you aren't hitting on them.

If you understand the rules of engagement upfront, you can be sensitive to an individual's feelings and proactively help that person accept your expression of gratitude and good feelings.

Practice acknowledgment with your spouse or significant other. When was the last time you told the most important person in your life how much he or she means to you and why? If it's been too long, or never, be prepared to get a weird stare or even some suspicion about your motives for saying something nice!

Think back to when you first started dating—you noticed every enchanting detail about this new special person in your life. In fact, you paid attention by *listening* attentively to every word. You thought your new partner was incredible, and said so—often. And you probably drove your friends and family nuts by telling them about all the great things your new love said and did!

Then you made a longer lasting commitment or got married, and all of a sudden when you got back to the business of your life, you stopped courting the one you love. I'm suggesting you start acknowledging your life's most valuable ally again with your words and deeds.

The most successful relationships remain so because both people continue to communicate their love, affection, and appreciation for their partners frequently. If you have children, you must tell them as often as you possibly can how much and why you love them. Look them straight in their eyes and give them great big hugs and lots of kisses. If you are fortunate enough to still have your parents, thank them for everything they've ever done for you. And tell them you love them in as many ways as you can think to do so, every chance you get.

I sincerely hope you start putting this advice into daily practice in your life beginning today. Pick up the phone, write a letter, send an email, leave the office early, and get yourself home. Tell each member of your family how much you cherish and love them.

As you begin to acknowledge the people in your life, you may notice that many individuals (even those closest to you) have a hard time receiving acknowledgment. For example, many straight American men are overly concerned about being seen as "macho." Unfortunately, this self-imposed or societal pressure to keep up a certain "tough guy" image often gets in the way of how a father and son relate to and communicate with one another. Don't let hang-ups rule your life or keep you from expressing your feelings to loved ones.

Remember to acknowledge all the very important people in your life. Include each member of your Circle of Success, your friends, coworkers, clients, neighbors, and any other special people who make your life better by being in it. Do this often and be specific.

Have you ever really stopped to notice the people who make your life more comfortable? If you live in an apartment building and hurry off to work each morning, do you ever smile and say good morning to your doorman? Do you really appreciate how hard most servers and bus-staff work when you're out dining with your friends?

How many people do you know who really appreciate their servers, hairdressers, delivery people, and all of the other men and women who work hard every day to make their lives easier? For most people, the practice of giving tips has become a form of acknowledgment, but "tips" started out as an acronym for To Insure Prompt Service.

When I frequent a particular restaurant, I make it a point to become friendly with the staff. I like to learn everyone's names, including the correct pronunciations. (If someone mispronounced your name, wouldn't you feel they considered you to be insignificant?) Over time, as I get to know certain staff members, I enjoy hearing about their families, lives, and aspirations. If Mario was out of work for several days, I'd be sure to welcome him back on his return and tell him I missed seeing him while he was gone. That's acknowledgment.

Unfortunately, most people don't pay attention to the people around them to the extent I describe. What happened to looking the person who greets you at the door in the eye? Are you afraid you might melt if you actually smiled and said hello as you passed by?

My friends and dinner guests are often amazed by the reception I get in restaurants. They can't believe I am so well liked simply because I ask people about their day or about how their child is doing in school. What some of my guests have failed to understand is that I really do take time to care about the people who take care of me. They know they matter to me because I remember the things that matter to them.

Acknowledgment is about learning how to understand and appreciate the people in your life. Have you ever met someone who made a powerful impression on you—so much so that you felt the need to say so? As someone who understands the value of networking, I am on a continual recruiting mission of sorts. When I meet people who strike me as a good fit for a non-profit organization I work with, a particular client's business, or a special project, I tell them.

Sometimes a complete stranger will look at me like they think I'm nuts for approaching them with such enthusiasm about one of my projects, clients, or causes. But usually, after I tell them how they impressed me, they are open to learning about the opportunity. I always make it a habit to exchange business cards or contact information so I can follow up. It continues to amuse me when people are truly shocked to hear from me because they didn't expect me to follow up!

Whenever I attend a charity event, I typically introduce myself to the keynote speakers and honorees. I like to acknowledge the things that struck a chord with me during their talks.

In one instance, I met a powerful New York City restaurateur after he gave a speech about the mistreatment of minorities in high-end restaurants. I talked with him about an article one of my classmates from Princeton had written about the racism he discovered when he went to work "undercover" at an exclusive country club. As a result of our conversation, I created a sensitivity training class for this restaurateur's staff and management—and we formed a relationship that led to some very successful events.

There are many nights when I am not attending black-tie galas. In fact, I often dine alone. One night when I was having dinner at a very busy Manhattan restaurant, I found myself seated next to a man, his wife, and his daughter who were visiting from out of town (I knew they weren't native New Yorkers because I overheard their strong Southern accents!). I also noticed an interesting appetizer they were enjoying and couldn't resist commenting that it looked really good. They kindly asked me if I'd like to try it, and we began talking.

The family was from Louisiana, and the gentleman was an attorney. We enjoyed conversing over our dinners and exchanged business cards before going our separate ways.

The next day, I put it on my To Do List to write the man a brief letter about how much I enjoyed meeting his family at dinner and that I looked forward to getting together when I travel to his part of the country. But he beat me to it. That day I received a long email from him acknowledging me! And, I have to tell you, it felt so good to receive that email.

Exercises

1. List ten people, and describe the difference they have made in your life.
2. Acknowledge your spouse/significant other daily.
3. Acknowledge two strangers per day for something special.

For their inspiration and guidance with the material in this chapter, many thanks go to:

Terry Ongaro. For offering your heart and teaching me about the power of love.

Rochelle Rachelson. For remembering every detail of what is important to all friends.

Nichole Wright. For being receptive and open to my coaching.

Gregg Epstein. For believing in my vision and demonstrating that maturity has no relationship to age.

Gabby Digiovannantonio. For making me feel very welcome at the Trump Marina Hotel and Casino by calling me "Buddy."

Wealthy Profile #9

Commercial real estate executive, 52, married with a twenty-eight-year-old daughter, a twenty-six-year-old daughter, and two grand-children. Lives in New York City. He recently sold his company for over $50 million. He encourages all of his senior executives to get involved with philanthropic causes as a requirement for advance-ment. He has given well over $10 million to various healthcare and Jewish causes over the past ten years. In an industry with question-able integrity, he is a man of utmost trustworthiness. He loves ten-nis, golf, fine dining, and art. He has met most of his business contacts through participating in his passions. He is a charismatic, fun-loving person who lives life to the fullest.

CHAPTER 17

Health, Vitality, and Fitness

On the surface, Thoreau's elegant, immortal words seem deceptively simple to follow: "Go confidently in the direction of your dreams. Live the life you've imagined . . ."

I wrote this book to share what I've learned from others who have boldly pursued their heart's passions and live life on their own terms. While I subscribe to Mr. Thoreau's philosophy wholeheartedly, *The Passion for Success* is not meant to conjure images of tranquility—the kind where you can see yourself enjoying a simple life by Walden Pond or singing "Kum Ba Ya" around a campfire.

This book is meant to serve as a WAKE-UP call for stressed-out people who have lost their way and want to remember their dreams. I hope you will use it is as a reference guide to:

- Get yourself back on track (as many times as necessary)
- Go for the life you want for yourself
- Become the person you've always wanted to be

Make no mistake about it; following your heart isn't for lightweights. Sustaining high levels of passion and success will require rigorous effort on your part. You will succeed if your intention is pure and your desire is strong enough (as long as you have the right tools and the staying power).

Up to this point, much attention has been focused on developing your "inner game." Now, let's spend time conditioning for the mindset of champions—the actions that prepare the mind and body for maximum performance.

Whether you are the type of person who tests the waters with your big toe or someone who dives in from the high platform, once you leave your safe harbor, you'll become more reliant on your mind and body to keep you afloat, especially when life's currents take you out into deeper, rougher, uncharted territories. When it's sink or swim, I always want to be in shape!

I also want to live long (and strong) enough to enjoy every precious moment when I finally realize each of my life's dreams. What's the point of literally killing yourself to sell your firm for millions of dollars, if you can't spend more time with family or see the world with friends because your heart, kidneys, lungs, or liver keep you bedridden?

Pop Quiz:

1. On a scale of 1 to 10, rate your overall physical condition.
2. Are you more than ten pounds overweight?
3. Do you know your Body Mass Index?
4. Do you know your resting heart rate?
5. When was the last time you checked your blood pressure?
6. How are your cholesterol levels?
7. Do you feel winded or a tightness in your chest climbing stairs?
8. Do you tire easily?
9. Are you always tired?
10. How many hours of sleep do you need at night to feel rested?
11. Have you ever had a mammogram or prostate exam, colonoscopy, and any other recommended health-related tests?
12. Do you drink too much, smoke, take sleeping pills, and/or any other drugs?
13. How many hours do you spend working out every week?
14. When was the last time you engaged in any form of exercise and broke a sweat?

15. Look back at the first question. Would you still rate
   yourself with the same number?

Health, vitality, and fitness enable and ensure our quality of
life.

In addition to making sure I can pass my own pop quiz with
flying colors, I measure my health by how well my immune system is functioning. I pay attention to my body's cues (e.g., di-
gestion, energy levels, ability to fight off colds, etc.).

Matters of basic health may seem trivial, but nothing
could be further from the truth. Unfortunately, the conventional wisdom among so many of the adults I meet is that all
we need to do is pop pills when our stomachs get upset after
overindulging; take aspirin when we have a mild ache somewhere; sip water and swallow a "sleep aid" when we suffer
with insomnia.

In our culture, we do whatever we can to stop the pain using the latest and greatest Western medicine has to offer. Sur-
prisingly, the majority of even the most highly educated people
I know fail to consider the long-term consequences of abusing
their bodies. They routinely take drugs to suppress the S.O.S.
messages their bodies send up in the form of headaches, irritable bowel syndrome, insomnia, chronic colds and infections,
even chest pains.

Do you have any idea how many liposuction and gastric by-
pass surgeries are performed every year? Where does it end?

If suddenly stopping all of your bad health habits is too
daunting for you right now, why not try adding one new good
habit? Drink one more glass of water every day. At the end of
one year, you'll have consumed 365 more glasses of water.

Water carries the body's toxins out with it. Every athlete
knows how critical proper hydration is to performance. When our
immune systems wear down and we're fighting a bad cold, virus,
or flu, the doctor's advice always includes drinking lots of fluids,
especially water. And, when massage therapists work those
"knots" out of our backs, they're actually breaking up toxins that
have built up in our muscles. The reason we are advised to drink
lots of water after a massage is to flush out all of those toxins.

If you want to learn more about how to live a healthier lifestyle, I highly recommend reading any book by Dr. Andrew Weil. A Harvard-educated M.D., Dr. Weil advocates "integrative medicine," which combines some of the practices of conventional medicine with preventative and natural healing. I also recommend books by Dr. Deepak Chopra and Wayne Dyer's CD, "Secrets of Your Own Healing Power." One of my favorite health and fitness writers is June Lay. Her website, www.junefit.com, is an excellent source of health, exercise, and weight-loss tips. Her site also offers some great recipes, so be sure to check it out!

This chapter is entitled, "Health, Vitality, and Fitness" because each one of these qualities is so vital to our ability to enjoy an extraordinary life. The terms *health* and *vitality* are not synonymous. *Vita* is the Latin word for "life," and vitality is energy. There are healthy people who lack vitality and vital people who aren't healthy.

Vitality generates the energy successful people depend upon to accomplish all of the things they set out to do in their lives. With vitality our blood seems to flow faster, our breaths seem to be deeper, and our sense of being alive emanates from something beyond our physical body's biological functioning.

Vitality is energy that manifests physically, but originates from our state of mind. Some very successful people also exude a charisma that feels like a very powerful positive energy. They'll smile when they tell you they have so much to do and never enough time. You'll never hear these people say they "just try to make it through the day" or they're "just killing time."

In addition to being a very attractive quality, vitality feeds the spirits of everyone around us—our children, coworkers, friends, and lovers. This inner energy force has the power to energize everyone who comes in contact with it.

Vital people are the polar opposite of the negativity-charged individuals who leave us feeling drained and depressed after we've been in their company.

Vitality seems to be a by-product of a general sense of well-being and faith in oneself and in life. It is an outgrowth of happiness, contentment, and love, not fear. Passionate people possess this very special brand of enthusiasm.

If I catch myself feeling down, I can pick myself back up in an instant when I tap into my own vitality.

If you are planning to begin living life several levels above where you are now, start cultivating vitality by eating right, exercising, and surrounding yourself with positive influences. The sooner you achieve this higher altitude attitude, the sooner you'll enjoy its benefits.

- You will feel more energized.
- Your mind will start thinking more clearly and quickly.
- People will look forward to seeing you (and will miss you when you're gone).
- You'll be more motivated (even to do things like walking the dog or cleaning your room).
- You'll want to play harder and sleep less.

Now, imagine how much more you could do if you added fitness into your life, too!

Fitness gives us the stamina required to sustain the life our vitality creates. Physical fitness elevates and promotes overall health. When we're fit, our immune systems are stronger so our bodies can fight illness and heal quicker.

The goal of cardiovascular fitness is to strengthen our hearts and lungs. How fast and far can you run, jog on a treadmill, or bike? How would you do in an aerobics class? Can you honestly tell yourself you are the picture of health, vitality, and wellness?

There is no question that when our bodies are in good shape we feel better. Athletes spend hours working out each and every day because they want to perform at their highest levels for as long as they possibly can. Of course they want to continually get better at their game, but most of their time and effort is spent on conditioning.

When Martina Navratilova first came onto the tennis scene, she was not a serious threat to the reigning queen of the court, Chris Evert. Even though she was still a teenager, Navratilova was out-of-shape and admittedly had terrible eating habits. I remember Navratilova's dramatic physical and mental transformation as she lost weight and body fat, gained muscle mass, and began winning more tennis matches. She got stronger, quicker, and even developed greater mental toughness.

Once Navratilova made up her mind to start acting like a champion, she was unstoppable. Not only did she elevate her own game, she raised the level of play in women's tennis. To win against her new rival, Evert found she had to finally come off the baseline, and she had to start hitting the gym!

Chris Evert's greatness came from her mental discipline. She was one of the most consistent champions to ever grace the tennis court. What made Evert extraordinary was her commitment to perfecting the ordinary. She wasn't the fastest or strongest female player on the women's circuit, but she was the toughest in her day. She possessed an incredible ability to concentrate on each point of every single game. She rarely lost her cool over a bad call because she knew the only thing that mattered was the final score.

Today's champions—both on and off the court—know they require every edge to achieve the pinnacle of success to which they aspire. They win more because they want to win more than everyone else, and they are willing to work harder than everybody else to condition their bodies and minds for winning.

What separates the champions who consistently win from the one-hit wonders? Invariably, at the highest levels of competition, a very slight differential in the amount of time committed to training can yield significantly higher rates of return.

Do you remember the story of the Steve Redgrave, the rower who won gold medals at five consecutive Olympic games over a twenty-year period? He trained one more day each year than each of his competitors—he never took off for Christmas!

Tiger Woods stays out on the green for an extra thirty minutes practicing his putting, but that doesn't seem to explain how he could win so much more than every other great golfer—until you consider the power of compounding thirty extra minutes of practice a day, year upon year.

Putting drills are so ordinary. Anybody could do them, right? Yet only extraordinary individuals discipline themselves to spend so much time practicing the ordinary. Within the elite ranks of the world's greatest champions, still fewer have the mental fortitude and desire to remain at the top for as long as their bodies will allow.

After winning his seventh Tour de France, Lance Armstrong lamented the fact that his body will never be in the same top physical condition because he won't continue to train at the level he trains at for competition. He told Larry King he'll only exercise for an hour or two each day from now on.

Have you ever once in your life worked out for two hours? If you answered "yes," when was the last time you did so?

The busiest people I know tell me they don't have time to go to the gym. And when it comes to the reasons people don't exercise, I've heard just about every excuse imaginable. Successful people live by the motto, "There are no excuses." Success is all about priorities and making choices. At one of the private schools near my home in Florida, when the teachers address their students about misconduct, they advise the children to *make better choices.*

Consider the results you would realize if you made the choice to eat a piece of fruit instead of a donut or muffin each day: an original glazed *Krispy Kreme* donut contains two hundred calories, whereas an average size apple has eighty calories. It is a scientific fact that if you consume 3500 fewer calories over a period of time (assuming your level of activity stays the same), you will lose one pound. If you do the math, you will see that over the course of one year, you would lose twelve and a half pounds simply by substituting an apple a day for those donuts.

Health, vitality, and fitness require your ongoing commitment to yourself. Only you can decide to make your well-being a priority. If you truly want to lead a successful and passionate life, poor lifestyle choices just won't make the cut. You've got to treat your body like a temple and have more self-respect.

I honor my body by treating it like my most precious possession—because my health is my wealth. My mental and physical health is the foundation from which everything else in my life is possible. This is why I practice yoga. The rigors of yoga stretch my muscles, require disciplined deep breathing that carries oxygen to every cell of my body, elevate my heart rate to levels that improve my cardio fitness, and make me sweat out my body's toxins.

In addition to drinking lots of water, I don't eat much red meat or chicken. I do eat lots of fish, fruits, vegetables, and raw foods. I do not drink alcohol, nor do I take drugs (not even caffeine). Ironically, I've met strangers who have asked me if I take drugs because they cannot believe the levels of energy I sustain.

Your Circle of Success can be instrumental in aiding your efforts to improve your health, vitality, and fitness. When you party with friends who like to drink too much or eat all the wrong foods, you're more likely to indulge. But if you surround yourself with healthy and fit people, you begin learning and adapting their habits.

My suggestion is to expand your Circle to include the kinds of people who will support your desire to optimize your health and well-being. If your closest friends and family aren't supportive of your commitment to better diet and lifestyle choices, you may find it necessary to skip certain types of gatherings that may be too tempting (e.g., barbeques, fish fries, happy hours, etc.) until your new choices solidify into habits.

I am also never too shy to approach someone at the gym or on the tennis court. I've said, "I noticed your workout. While I'm not at your level, I'd love to learn what it is that you're doing [with your serve, your weights, etc.] because I would really like to try to incorporate some of your technique into my workout."

Successful people have learned to overcome their shyness. You can do it, too. You have nothing to lose and everything to gain—your acknowledgment will make that person feel terrific, and you create an opportunity to learn something new (and you might make a new friend).

Finally, do not underestimate the power of desire. It is the life force and the source of our motivation. Champions know how to tap into their desire and channel it with greater consistency than others. Champions also realize they need to call upon their desire to win not only in the critical moment of the big game, but in each lonely, boring, ordinary moment that will lead to each first place victory.

Champions are not one-hit wonders who can be written off

as lucky. Even if you believe all you need is more luck in your life, then consider this: Luck = Opportunity + Preparation.

This chapter has focused on the steps you can take to better prepare for your success. Health, vitality, and fitness will not last forever (and may not exist for you today), especially if you've neglected yourself. Please do not take your health and well-being for granted. You've only been given one precious body to care for, so make the commitment today to begin treating it as your most valuable possession.

Exercises

1. For ten consecutive days, do a cardiovascular exercise for twenty minutes (preferably in the morning).
2. For thirty days, drink one gallon of water each day, and notice the change in your energy and physique.
3. Write a description of your ideal body (weight, waist size, body fat, etc.)

For their inspiration and guidance with the material in this chapter, many thanks go to:

Robin Gillman. For your commitment to having a great body and going to the gym every day no matter what.

June Lay. For your weekly fitness and nutrition "tips" at junefit.com.

Elizabeth Koch. For your lessons on eating small meals seven times per day.

Rob Endelman. For your participation in multiple sports events on the same day in East Hampton.

Tony Peyser. For your great fitness level and willingness to begin surfing late in life.

Wealthy Profile #10

Investment banker, 48, married with a fifteen-year-old son and a thirteen-year-old daughter. Lives in New York City. He was a very successful trader at a major New York City investment bank and left to start his own firm twelve years ago. He has worked with his wife to build one of the largest African-American-owned investment banking companies in the world. He and his wife are committed to empowering African Americans to achieve greatness. They do this by sitting on the boards of several large non-profit organizations. He has grown his business methodically and thus has a solid, uncompromising foundation. He inspires many young African Americans to pursue a career in investment banking by speaking in schools and providing internships at his firm. He enjoys playing basketball, exercising, and fine dining, and he makes sure that he participates in his children's lives.

CHAPTER 18

Children as Masters of Life and Teachers of Truth

One of the greatest fallacies of all time is that our children need us to guide them to truth. Children are born with more intelligence than we give them credit for. They can teach us things about life and ourselves that we never knew or have long forgotten.

Watch how children play and interact with each other. They are completely open to experiencing everything and everyone just as they are. Every time I see my little brothers, I think about how incredible it is that they are filled with so much love and acceptance. Whenever we play together, I can remember myself as a child filled with excitement, curiosity, and vitality—all that great energy.

We adults are the ones who teach children the lessons about life that ultimately spoil their natural states of joy and unconditional love. And, without meaning any harm, we often say and do things that stifle our children, their enthusiasm, and their passion for life.

When I was a kid there was a common expression, "Children are to be seen and not heard." Today, I hear parents admonishing their children to use their "inside voices" when they take their kids out to a restaurant or anywhere else where kids can't be kids. It's natural for children to get excited, feel giddy, and even shout enthusiastically when they want to get your attention because they have something they want to share with you.

Whenever I hear someone use that awful expression, I shudder and think about Archie Bunker telling his wife Edith to "stifle it." Stifling someone's excitement and self-expression is damaging.

If we want our children to thrive in this world, we must do everything in our power to encourage and develop their innate enthusiasm for life. Kids just want to keep playing. They want to meet new people and have fun. They have so much energy that it feels so good to them when they can run, jump, and let it all out!

Children never want to miss anything, so they never want to go to sleep. My little brothers are a perfect example: when bedtime comes around they plead for "five more minutes." They'll say, "Please, read just one more story," or ask, "Can we play this game just one more time?"

Where does all of our energy go when we become adults? If we're bigger than our kids, shouldn't we have more energy than they do? At what point in our lives does our desire to stay up all night switch over to wanting more and more sleep? When do we stop wanting just five more minutes?

I think the answer to the last question is simple: We were told "No" by our parents over and over until we just stopped asking.

When I come into the office in the morning and the first thing someone says is, "Oh, I'm so tired," I immediately think to myself that this person isn't excited about his job. Do you recognize the person I'm talking about? If you see yourself in this scenario, let me ask you another question: If you won two all-expense-paid tickets to anywhere and it was 4:00 a.m. the morning of your trip, would you feel tired? Probably not. In fact, you'd be so excited that you wouldn't be able to sleep the night before. When we're not happy and we don't feel enthusiastic about our future, we start to feel tired all the time.

Kids are excited about each day. They can't wait for tomorrow and the next day and the next day. They can't wait for school to start . . . they can't wait for summer . . . they can't wait for their birthdays . . . they can't wait for the Fourth of July!

I remember the feeling I'd get the night before Christmas. My parents would try to get my brothers and me to go to sleep (so Santa could put our gifts under the tree), but we wanted to stay up to see Santa! Even when we couldn't keep our eyes open any longer and we'd fall asleep, we'd wake up throughout the night just to see if it was morning yet.

On Christmas Day when it was time to open our presents, we'd rip the wrapping off each gift and start screaming, "It's a Matchbox car!" or "I got a new bike!"

What happens along the way to adulthood that even when we receive a gift we're not happy? How many times have you heard an adult say, "Oh, I don't like this color," or, "I told you I wanted the *Polo* shirt." When did labels become so important? (Kids don't care about labels.) How did we get so jaded?

Somewhere on our journey to adulthood we lose sight of our hopes and dreams. We give up on life and go through the motions of living; we do just enough to survive.

Yet, we are all born into this world as bundles of pure energy. Our parents love us and do the best they can to raise us to live in this world. But our parents also make lots of mistakes, just like their parents did with them. If you are a parent, you've probably made more than your share of mistakes, too.

For better and for worse we become just like our parents. We learn their habits, the good ones and the bad ones. We take on their attitudes and follow their examples, just as they taught us to do. Sadly, parents pass on their own insecurities and prejudices to their children. I saw a perfect example of this in Central Park one day last year. As I was passing by a playground, I saw a group of children playing in a sandbox. They were all about four and five years of age. These kids were having a great time just being kids. I laughed as I watched them throwing sand at each other, building things, laughing, and chatting, and just full-out playing.

As I continued to enjoy watching the kids in the sandbox, I noticed another little boy walk over to the sandbox so he could play with the other kids. Suddenly, one of the mothers (a well-dressed woman) called to her son, who was already busily playing in the sand, "It's time to go now." When the boy kept asking why, his mother repeatedly replied, "We have to go now."

I immediately knew why this mother wanted to leave the park. Did I mention that the little boy who wanted to join the other kids in the sandbox was Black? This noticeably affluent woman didn't want her child to make friends with someone who was different. Not only was this boy Black, but I could see from the way he was dressed that he didn't come from a family with much means.

I noticed these things because I'm an adult. But do you think the kids in the sandbox saw what that mother and I saw? Of course not! For those kids, this little boy was another new playmate for the afternoon—one more kid to laugh with, throw sand, and have fun.

Kids just want to play. They don't care how much money someone has or what kind of car a person drives. They don't read the labels on your clothes, handbags, shoes, and jewelry. We adults teach our kids that all of those things matter every time we measure a person's worth by adding up all of their symbols of status.

We have so much to learn from our kids . . .

When children see a person of a different race for the first time they say the darnedest things! We laugh because they speak the truth—the most beautiful, innocent truth.

They don't fear people who look different or talk with a different accent (or speak in a foreign language). They learn hate and fear from adults. Why can't adults learn love, acceptance, and fearlessness from children? Children are innately open, inclusive, curious and excited about diversity. If you are one of those adults who picked up some ugly habits and prejudices from the adults in your life, it's not too late to change if you want to become a better human being.

Adopting a more open-minded attitude and embracing people of different backgrounds will give you a broader perspective, a richer life, and set a positive example for your own children. Sometimes it's a good idea to leave your clique behind and make some new friends. Nothing could be easier than pursuing the things you love doing and meeting all types of people who share your interests.

As you begin to expand your horizons and Circle of Success,

I hope you'll choose to see the world in all of its brilliant hues and hear its most exotic voices calling to you.

Many of the parents I meet through business, philanthropy, and tennis send their kids cross-country or to Europe when they graduate from high school. They tell me this is so important for their kids' development because it gives them an appreciation for what they have. Every kid I meet who has been given this opportunity does come back with an entirely new perspective on life.

I'm suggesting that you also need a new perspective. When was the last time you stepped out of your comfort zone? Why not get out from behind your walls and beyond the end of your driveway? Venture beyond the borders of your hometown to see more of the state, country, and world in which you live.

While you'll have to make a conscious effort to follow this advice, your children won't. They can't wait to get out and see what's going on in the world around them. They want to see, do, and learn about everything new. They may not always love school, but I assure you they love learning. You've probably said it yourself, "Kids are like sponges—they soak up everything." That's why when they're small, they repeat every new word they hear—even when we don't want them to!

So why is it that when we graduate from school we stop learning? Someone told me the average male will read only two books after he graduates from college—two books! If that's true, it is a pathetic statistic.

I wonder where adults lose their desire to keep learning. Could it be in our educational system? Rather than inspiring our children to love reading and promoting the value of learning, our schools have gotten caught up in teaching kids how to get higher standardized test scores. What happened to teaching kids how to think for themselves, how to develop their creativity, how to analyze a fact pattern, and how to offer their critical opinions? Our educational institutions are stifling the potential and creativity of our future generations in order to mass produce graduates using fewer resources—fewer teachers, no art, no sports and fewer classrooms.

I'm sure when our kids add everything together they learn

precisely where education falls on society's priority list. If you disagree with my conclusions about the current state of education because you are doing your part, let's review your methodology: Do you make sure your kids do all of their homework assignments? Do you *help* them with their homework or do you *do* their homework for them?

I urged you to stop doing your kids' homework because they need to get the answers for themselves if they are to become independent adults. You've got to be stronger than your children. At first, they'll beg, plead, and throw tantrums, but once you get past the painful initial withdrawal of enabling your kids, you'll discover the marvelous intelligence your children have within them. This may be the single most empowering act you ever do for your children. Please have faith in what I'm telling you and have faith in your kids.

If you've been using homework time as your only one-on-one time with your children, I suggest you find other more appropriate ways to spend time together. In my family, we played all sorts of games. Our parents played Scrabble, chess, backgammon, Risk, bridge, and so many other games with us. It was our family's time to relate to one another, compete, and have fun all together. I also remember playing basketball with my brothers on our driveway and ping-pong and air hockey in our basement. After school and on weekends, our parents always gave us some time to be kids.

Today, children have less time with their parents and their own brothers and sisters. They keep schedules that would exhaust any adult:

Monday:	Soccer practice
Tuesday:	Karate
Wednesday:	Music lessons
Thursday:	Math tutoring
Friday:	Swim team
Sat/Sun:	Religious instruction

What happened to allowing kids to have some down time? It was in these moments that we had time to think for ourselves. We invented new games with our imaginations, organized spontaneous "pick-up" basketball or stickball games with our siblings and neighbors, read a book, or climbed a tree in the safety of our own backyard.

We learn as much or more about the joy of being alive in these moments than we ever do in the classroom. And kids get an entirely different experience when they organize their own baseball games without any intervention from adults, than when they compete in organized sports. They need the opportunity to experience some of both.

Playing tennis, I get to talk with a lot of teenagers and young adults wherever I go. Far too many of these young people tell me they never really liked tennis, but their parents wanted them to learn the game. Even though tennis is my number one passion and a fabulous sport, I'll be the first to ask someone why they're spending time doing something they really don't enjoy.

Some kids and many parents will tell me they think tennis is a good way to meet the "right people." Or they're hoping if their children work hard enough at it, they'll earn a scholarship to a good school. What happened to tennis being a game? What happened to letting our kids be kids? What happened to giving our children time to play and have fun?

Is it any wonder that our kids are growing up to become just like us—playing it safe, choosing a career based on how much money they'll earn, forgetting how to relate to their family and friends with the same smiles, laughter, and joy they had when they played in the sandbox.

What are we afraid will happen if we let our children follow their passions in life? Are we worried they will foolishly head down a dangerous path leading to their premature death or ruin? Isn't it possible that your children are smart enough, talented enough, and perhaps even spoiled enough to figure out how to get everything they want in life?

Imagine if you were brave enough to let go and allowed your children to find out what it is they really want to do with their lives. What if your children are still doing what they love fifteen or twenty years from now? Do you have any idea how magnificently fulfilling your precious sons' and daughters' lives would be if you could teach them how to follow their dreams?

Do children need basic instruction, lots of guidance, and nurturing as they grow to adulthood? Absolutely! It is our responsibility to teach our little ones how to swim so they won't drown. We need to explain to them that if they put their hand on a hot stove they can get burned. It is up to us to do everything in our power to keep them safe from harm, but it's just as important to let our kids fall, make mistakes, get hurt, and deal with disappointment and failure. These are the lessons all children must learn for themselves in order to develop and grow into self-sufficient, self-confident, strong, wise, and productive adults. If we have the wisdom and restraint to teach our children in this way, we will raise men and women who are kind and loving because they are happy and secure.

It is only natural that we want what's best for our children. We want them to have everything we didn't have. They rely on us to protect, guide, and love them even when they become adults. I'm suggesting we get out of their way just enough to give them room to spread their wings and see how high they can fly.

When you catch yourself doing your child's homework, insisting they will thank you for giving them piano lessons, or telling them to forget about being an artist because they'll never make any money at it, STOP yourself.

The next time your son or daughter asks you how to spell a vocabulary word, tell your child you have a gift for him or her. Then, go into your desk drawer and take out the gift-wrapped present you have been waiting to give at this moment. As you hand over the gift, give your child a big hug and kiss on the forehead. Be sure your child reads your handwritten note before unwrapping your special gift.

My dear son/daughter,
I know I don't tell you enough, but I am so proud of how well you are doing and I have so much faith in your abilities. I hope you will use this gift to find some of the answers to the questions you ask me, because I want you to know where you can find them for yourself. Always remember, I will be right here to guide and encourage you.
Love,
Mom/Dad

When they see the gift is a dictionary, they'll probably *forget* to thank you for the moment. But they'll remember your gift for the rest of their lives.

Exercises

1. Spend one hour per week with a child who is under the age of five and observe his or her behavior. Write down your findings.
2. Do something that you consider "silly" for ten consecutive days.
3. Draw a picture of your ideal life with crayons, and ask a child under age ten to critique it and tell you what they see.

For their inspiration and guidance with the material in this chapter, many thanks go to:

Justin Roth. For teaching your father to take risks in business.

Danyelle Shapiro. For teaching me to be punctual and spontaneous.

Earl Graves. For creating an environment for your children to grow your already successful business.

Lindsay Mure. For creating the foundation of Life's Passions Events Planning with your ambition at age nineteen.

Ari and Ravi Eaton. For teaching my father the joy of being a parent late in life.

CHAPTER 19

Creating an Extraordinary Future

Ordinary is for the other ninety-nine percent. After a brief childhood, which they can't even remember, ordinary people grow up and get to work. They have kids of their own, follow the rules (set by others), and use the same routine day in and day out . . . until retirement day comes. Then, shortly thereafter, they die.

Extraordinary people never forget how to approach life with the same energy and enthusiasm as children. They follow their dreams, take risks, make mistakes and always stay true to their hearts' passions.

Extraordinary people never follow others. They know their happiness won't come from keeping up with the Jones', their wealth won't come from punching a clock or investing with the rest of the market, and they make their own rules and define their own success.

As we conclude our exploration of *The Passion for Success—The Mindset of Champions*, we will review several of the principles presented herein. These are the same ideas and ideals I am striving to incorporate into my own life. I hope they serve and guide you as you move forward on your road to an infinitely more fulfilling life.

One certainty I've already discovered is that you won't be able to live a purpose-driven life staying on autopilot. Realizing your life's potential and making an impact on humanity require your active participation. Just going through the motions won't cut it.

In Chapter 5, we looked at finding your purpose in life. If

you know your life's purpose, are you doing what you need to accomplish it? If you still need to figure this out for yourself, try closing your eyes and envisioning your last hour on earth: What do you hope your loved ones will say as they remember your life and the kind of person you've been?

Keeping your eyes closed, spend some time thinking about that *life line* between the day you were born and the day you die, (that *hyphen* I asked you to remember in Chapter 2).

When you open your eyes, get out a pad of paper and a good pen, and start writing down everything you need to do to live the life of the person you know you can be.

If you still aren't sure about your purpose in life after you try these exercises, I suggest you ask, "What's my purpose?" each night before you fall asleep.

Keep watching and listening for the answers to come from your everyday life. Pay attention to recurring themes that may contain the messages you might dismiss if you're preoccupied or looking in the wrong places.

Change the questions you ask. Rather than asking, "Why is it that I never get what I want?" or, "Why didn't my parents give me more?" or, "Why is he always so lucky" or, "Why did God let this happen to me?" ask better questions, such as:

- What is the lesson to be learned here?
- Who am I being that I am allowing this to happen?
- What good can come from this experience?

Don't let your pain paralyze you. Use this emotion to spring you into motion. I channel the pain I feel from losing my mother to cancer to give me energy to fight against the disease. I continue to seek opportunities to raise money for research and other related activities that can make a difference in the lives of patients and their families.

What moves you to the point of wanting to change what is happening around you? Be mindful of the power and empowerment that come through faith. Take enough time to clear your mind, find your center, and regain your balance every single day. Meditate for at least fifteen minutes a day and say your prayers. Prayer isn't about asking for things. It's about offering our thanks for the abundance already present in our lives. It's also a means of asking the questions that will lead us to the answers we seek to become better human beings. Begin your meditation each day by acknowledging all of the people and things for which you are grateful.

Reach out to others. An extraordinary life cannot take place without extraordinary relationships. Spend more time with your family. What's the point of getting married and having children, if you are not going to be present in their lives?

Listen, comfort, and enrich the lives of your partner, children, parents, siblings, friends, and coworkers. Do one good deed for someone else every day. Write it down and add a deposit slip to your own "matzo" box.

Find your soul mate and share your dreams together. Keep sharing your dreams with the people who will hold you accountable (your Circle of Success) to become the extraordinary individual you want to be.

Have more fun. Life is too short to be so serious all the time. Watch how kids play, and pay attention to what makes them laugh. Climb a tree with your nephews and nieces; help them build their treehouse.

Loosen up. Say something outrageous at a cocktail party and encourage others to make it a night you'll all remember.

Live each day to its fullest. My mother and too many people I knew died prematurely.

Take more risks. Chapter 12 reminds us that every successful person takes risks. The trick is in learning how to better assess and manage the risks we take.

Find the courage to overcome the fears that keep you from experiencing the extraordinary. Staring down and defeating our fears is incredibly exhilarating and empowering! What would you try if you knew you couldn't fail?

Act in a manner consistent with your beliefs and values. If you need to get clear on what you believe and what's important to you, do so. Don't delay; you cannot find your way without a moral compass.

Keep your word. I know I am far from perfect, but each day

I wake up and I do my best to honor the promises and obligations I've made to myself and the people in my life. And each night I remind myself that practicing the basic fundamentals makes people extraordinary.

So, what still stands between you and your ability to realize your life's dreams?

Have you figured out the answer to, "What am I doing with my gift of life?" Did you decide whether you want to be rich or wealthy?

What shape is your Life Plan Portfolio in? Could you yield higher returns by redistributing the time you've allotted to each of your life assets?

Don't forget my 10 Keys to Independence:

1. Live in the moment.
2. Create an exciting vision of the future.
3. Surround yourself with people who have what you want.
4. Keep your word.
5. Make unreasonable requests.
6. Give with no expectation of getting.
7. Take action every day consistent with your vision.
8. Trust in a Higher Power.
9. Be enthusiastic.
10. Be persistent.

Someday, we'll all be worm food. Stop trying to kill time, and start living in the moment! Figure out what you're passionate about (by trial and error) and spend more time doing each of those things with the people who mean the most to you. Resist the temptation to take the path of least resistance because you will never achieve lasting happiness and contentment by settling and playing it safe.

Model success and you will become successful. And be willing to do what unsuccessful people are unwilling to do.

In Chapter 4, I encouraged you to surround yourself with the people who can help you to achieve your goals. You must be extremely selective to choose individuals with high integrity who will always raise you up. Don't allow yourself to get dragged down by a pot of crabs. Sometimes it will be necessary to trade players on your team or ask to be traded as you seek to realize your life's full potential.

What perfect picture do you have framed in your mind? Do you feel happy and content whenever that picture comes to mind? Does it represent the reality you live today or is it a reminder of the distant past? We experience happiness in the present moment. Contentment is the ability to carry that happiness through from moment to moment.

As you reconnect with all of the most important people in your life, remember to check in with them from time to time. Ask them how they think you are doing in your relationship with one another. And, every once in a while, ask them what more you could do for them.

The most highly successful people possess the ability to focus. In Chapter 7, we looked at how to develop this essential skill and apply it to every dimension of our lives. Keep your children, family, and friends in clear focus—never lose sight of what ultimately matters most in this life so you won't lose your way.

Every now and then try listening to a new radio station, put a new CD into your car stereo, turn up the volume, and change up your rhythm. Learn new dance steps, sing in the shower, join your loved ones on the dance floor, and just let yourself go. When it comes to experiencing joy, there ain't nothing like it!

If you sincerely want to attract wealth into your life, let your money flow. Don't wait until you accumulate more. Get into the habit of giving your time and money now. Make philanthropy a passion.

Don't forget to do each of the exercises to build the self-esteem muscle as outlined in Chapter 11. Become best friends with the person you see in the mirror every morning with the "You're great" greeting. Do yourself a favor and don't skip this one.

I told you about a man named George Plimpton and the list he created of the one hundred things he wanted to accomplish in his lifetime. Each item on his list required some level of risk. I dare you to follow Mr. Plimpton's example. Make your own list and then set out to achieve as many of these challenges as you can during your lifetime.

Have faith in yourself. Whenever you have doubts, remember what my grandmother always told me: "we have the power to change our lives by altering our thoughts." If you are facing a challenge that no one else has overcome before you, remember that Roger Bannister showed the world that it was possible to run a mile in less than four minutes. You have abilities and an inner strength you haven't yet begun to tap.

When you learn to have faith in others, you will give them the gift of empowerment. Stop treating people like they are weak or unable to do for themselves. Show your children how much you believe in them, and practice a *guided letting go*. Give them the gift of independence and allow them to find their own self-confidence.

Take a good look at the people around you. Note where they are in each of the following areas in their life, to see where you will be five years from now (if your relationships stay the same):

- Overall health and fitness
- Education
- Financial success
- Spiritual development
- Interest in philanthropy
- Closeness to family
- Friendships
- Passion for success

Acknowledge every very important person in your life. Tell your children, as often as you possibly can, how much and why you love them. If your parents are alive, thank them, and tell them you love them every time you say good-bye.

Call, write a letter, or send an email to let the people who have made a difference in your life know how much you appreciate them.

Please do yourself a favor and make your health, vitality, and fitness a priority in your life. Stop abusing your body and start taking better care of yourself.

Make better choices.

Recognize the wisdom of our children. Watch how children play. Watch how kids open their presents. Kids don't care about how much money people have or what kinds of cars others drive. They don't notice the labels on your clothes and accessories. They measure another kid's worth by how well that kid plays with others. Children don't discriminate. They're excited to meet new and different people of all shapes, sizes, and colors. Learn love, acceptance, and fearlessness from your children. Keep learning from these incredible teachers, and play with your kids as often as you can. Be silly. Snuggle when you read bedtime stories together. Share your hopes and dreams. And fight for the cherry on top of the cake!

Live an extraordinary life filled with love and laughter that sets an example for your children to follow.

Exercises

1. What are two major life decisions you will make after completing this book?
2. Make a list of at least five people who would benefit from reading the book.
3. Let us know how we can help you live an extraordinary life!

For their inspiration and guidance with the material in this chapter, many thanks go to:

Douglas Gribin. For believing in me and supporting my life insurance business.

Bernadett Fejszes. For being the love of my life and my soulmate.

Bryan Rudnick. For being the Chief Operating Officer for all of my ventures and someone I can always count on.

Jonathan Rosen. For being a role model and a source of knowledge.

God. Without You, I would not be.

Wealthy Profile #11

Corporate CEO, 54, married with an eighteen-year-old son and a sixteen-year-old daughter. Lives in New York City. He has been a corporate executive his entire career and has risen through sheer determination, hard work, and the ability to inspire others. He is one of the few African Americans in history to achieve his level of success in corporate America. He loves tennis, running, fine dining, and reading. His demanding travel schedule makes it very challenging to spend time with his family; however, he has been able to structure his life in such a way that when he is with his family, there are no business interruptions. He is on the board of four philanthropic causes, which are focused on creating a positive environment for young African Americans. His fellow executives consistently talk about his focus, compassion, and visionary qualities. He came from modest means but always believed that anything was possible.

L'Chiam—To Life!
David Roy Eaton
August 2006

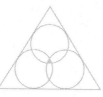

Notes

Chapter 11

1. *WordNet,* 2.0, (Princeton: Princeton University, 2003), s.v. "self-esteem."
2. ibid., s.v. "self-confidence."

Chapter 12

1. Ed Clayton, *Martin Luther King, Jr: The Peaceful Warrior* (New York: Pocket Books, 1968).

Chapter 13

1. Maya Angelou, "Eric Butterworth," *Eric Butterworth Foundation,* www.ericbutterworth.com/html/eric_bio.html (accessed August 9, 2006).
2. Oprah Winfrey, "Article Title," *O Magazine,* May/June 2000.

Invest in Yourself and Your Team

Does your organization have a meeting event, conference, or management retreat that needs to introduce a Passion for Success? David Roy Eaton may be the perfect solution for your keynote, breakout session or class.

David Roy Eaton brings high-energy and proven experience to your group with his training and message tailored to your audience. A perfect way to introduce a new Passion for Success initiative.

For more information, availability, and fees, please contact:

David Roy Eaton
Life's Passions Events Planning, LLC
2385 Executive Center Drive, Suite 100
Boca Raton, FL 33431
561-962-2766
speaking@lifespassions.com
www.thepassionfund.com